Twitter Marketing

How to Convert Your Twitter Followers Into Business Dollars

(Proven Business Strategy With a Simple Social Media to Earn Passive Income)

Paul Mitchell

Published By **Oliver Leish**

Paul Mitchell

All Rights Reserved

Twitter Marketing: How to Convert Your Twitter Followers Into Business Dollars (Proven Business Strategy With a Simple Social Media to Earn Passive Income)

ISBN 978-1-77485-947-6

No part of this guidebook shall be reproduced in any form without permission in writing from the publisher except in the case of brief quotations embodied in critical articles or reviews.

Legal & Disclaimer

The information contained in this ebook is not designed to replace or take the place of any form of medicine or professional medical advice. The information in this ebook has been provided for educational & entertainment purposes only.

The information contained in this book has been compiled from sources deemed reliable, and it is accurate to the best of the Author's knowledge; however, the Author cannot guarantee its accuracy and validity and cannot be held liable for any errors or omissions. Changes are periodically made to this book. You must consult your doctor or get professional medical advice before using any of the suggested remedies, techniques, or information in this book.

Upon using the information contained in this book, you agree to hold harmless the Author from and against any damages, costs, and expenses, including any legal fees potentially resulting from the application of any of the information provided by this guide. This disclaimer applies to any damages or injury caused by the use and application, whether directly or indirectly, of any advice or information presented, whether for breach of contract, tort, negligence, personal injury, criminal intent, or under any other cause of action.

You agree to accept all risks of using the information presented inside this book. You need to consult a professional medical practitioner in order to ensure you are both able and healthy enough to participate in this program.

TABLE OF CONTENTS

Chapter 1: Organic and Paid Twitter

In this book, I'll use the terms Paid Twitter and Organic Twitter in accordance with these definitions. Organic Twitter is any part of Twitter that isn't hosted on ads.twitter.com. Paid Twitter is any portion of your Twitter that is hosted on ads.twitter.com.

Let's look at the pertinent distinctions here by addressing a few questions. First, which one is best for me? Third, how do I get them to cooperate?

Organic or Paid - Which one is the best to Me and My Business?

There's no reason you shouldn't take advantage of the powerful and free tool called Organic Twitter. However, to clarify things If you can answer "yes" to any of these questions, you should be making use of organic Twitter.

1.) Does your target audience or customers has an active presence online on Twitter? i.e. do they tweet every day.

2.) Does your company's image lack an audience that is mass-market? i.e. Are over 50% of the potential customers unaware of your company, brand or product?

3.) Does customer feedback or conversations benefit your company?

The first reason is fairly simple, but I'll go over on the second and third.

Does your Brand have a limited mass-market reach?

If more than 50percent of your audience is aware of the name of your business, (the total amount of people who are using your product or service) Then you don't require Organic Twitter to increase awareness. But, and this is an enormous but, using the Twitter's free platform can be a valuable tool to connect with your current customers, regardless of the degree to which they are aware of your name. Twitter is among the biggest and possibly most user-friendly platforms around the globe.

However well-known your brand is, Twitter is instrumental for engaging with your audience.

I see a negative answer to this question to be more of an insight into the direction of your business as opposed to an absolute reason not to utilize Twitter naturally. When you are already a part of a large brand awareness, don't fret too much about building brand recognition and instead, utilize Twitter to provide feedback from customers tool. Be involved and attempt to influence conversations that already take place regarding your business. Wendy's (@Wendys) is one of the best examples of this. They draw on the infamous rivalries with other large brands to create humorous jokes that are extremely enthralling.

Would customer feedback or conversations Help your business?

Based on the transparency of Twitter, there's nothing that's more valuable for business than the unfiltered feedback of your customers. Twitter is the ideal platform to do this. It's free to connect with anyone and everywhere, and it's a public platform, meaning that all interactions are documented. Are you able to provide some great feedback about a new product release? Retweet, quote or retweet it and put it at on top of your timeline to ensure that anyone who is looking for your tweet will see it first.

Twitter is the best platform to provide immediate feedback.
If you don't have a response to 1 and 3, then you're distinct, and possibly B2B or enterprise in that sense. The absence of Twitter likely won't harm you however I would still suggest using it if you intend to use ads since it adds an additional level of authenticity to the platform that helps your account appear more credible.
I have worked with a variety of companies while working as an adviser to advertisers on Twitter and many of these were related to subscription boxes. Two kinds of companies always came up. Businesses with a presence, and those without an active presence. I was associated with one brand, let's call it NewBoxCo that was extremely present on Twitter. Always tweeting new customers or existing

customers to solicit feedback, or responding to positive or negative feedback. If they ran an advertisement they would receive hundreds of retweets or likes just because they'd established an following on Twitter. The algorithm would reward these tweets, and the price per impression, click, etc. will always be low.

Understanding Twitter's Strengths and Weaknesses

There are many ways to promote your business on. Each of them has strengths. The area where Twitter distinguishes itself is its capacity to reach a large audience and to spread its message quickly. The reason for this is two aspects which other platforms don't offer. Twitter is open and active. Because of these two aspects I've found that those trying to raise awareness of their brand or initiate a discussion around an issue would get the most effective results on Twitter. I'll go into more detail about the best ways to achieve these objectives in section 3.

What makes Twitter is different is its ability to reach a large audience and to spread the word quickly.

The other side on the other side is Direct Response advertising or "DR". This is the area where Twitter has had a difficult time over the years. The majority of advertisers who want to drive downloads, conversions and purchases and downloads, etc. frequently discover Twitter difficult and frustrating in comparison against Google and Facebook. However, that doesn't mean DR isn't feasible on Twitter however it is. This kind of advertising isn't one of Twitter's strengths . It will require a lot of effort for the advertiser to get satisfactory results.

Chapter 2: The Marketing Funnel On Twitter

Twitter's strengths could be in the area of brand recognition and building conversations however, that doesn't mean that it isn't possible to interact with potential customers in the various stages of the funnel. This chapter will show the areas where Twitter best fits into the picture and how you can make the most of Twitter in the various stages in the funnel.

How do you define a marketing funnel?

In essence it is the method that potential customers follow throughout their interaction with your company. The initial step is typically the discovery of or awareness of the existence of your business. The final step is typically acquisition , such as signing up or purchasing.

The Function for a Marketing Funnel

It's difficult to imagine being lost and finding your way back without a map, isn't it? You can think of the funnel as a map to your marketing strategy. It can be useful when you're creating campaigns, optimizing campaigns , or looking over the effectiveness of your campaigns.

I have a very general version of the funnel for marketing. There are many different versions available and I would advise you to research the different ones. To the greatest extent this will be a good choice for any campaign that you create through Twitter.

The funnel has four phases. The first step is awareness. The next is engagement, then consideration the third and conversion comes final. Below, I'll go over each and explain how Twitter can fit into each.

Awareness - Twitter's Best Stage

The first stage is concerned with making that first impression to potential clients who are yet to purchase or utilize your product or service. Twitter is extremely effective in the first stage. Being active and visible means connecting and interacting with your clients is fast and simple.

The importance of Awareness - It's obvious that sharing information about your company is crucial. One mistake I've seen many marketers making is that they combine the awareness stage with an additional stage of the funnel. In order to avoid it, you must follow this gentle(wo)man's rule.

Make sure to introduce yourself prior to soliciting someone to take actions for you or your company.

Imagine that you are looking at a beautiful girl or a boy at a friend's dinner event. The first thing that would be spoken out be to invite for an evening date? Most likely not. You should introduce yourself first, then get acquainted with them, and then determine if they are an ideal connection. This same principle applies advertising. You already know what person who is viewing your advertisement is to be based on the target you selected. The person however isn't sure the reason they're being targeted by you. Make sure you define the importance of your brand by introducing yourself.

There are three steps to set up your strategy for Becoming aware on Twitter:

Step 1.) Determine Your Audience (ask yourself the questions below)

Who are thought leaders in your field?

- Who's following these thought-leaders and what key words are they employing?

Who is on Twitter engaged with these hashtags and keywords? You can find people who retweet these thought people.

Step 2) Understand Your Audience

Are there any popular words that non-thought leaders do not use?

What hashtags drive the highest amount of Retweets and likes?

-- Does your audience share a bio description? Ex: "Mommy Blogger"

Step 3.)

-All of these keywords and hashtags are able to be targeted via Twitter ads, which is why you should be sure to keep these hashtags!

The thought-leader's Twitter accounts are ideal for focusing Follower's attention.

It's all about identifying the people you want to target with your ad campaigns. Important to consider is the keywords, thought leaders , etc. could also aid in targeting other platforms, too.

How to Increase Awareness with advertisements on Twitter The most important thing to do with an awareness advert is to simplify your brand's image into a concise, short sentence or image. Don't attempt to convert your audience or create an email list. Just tell your audience about what you offer.

The only action a user is required to take is to click on your advertisement to read more about your website, or to respond, like, or retweet on your post.

There are several campaigns that are effective for generating attention on Twitter. Awareness, tweet engagement & video campaigns all drive awareness.

Awareness If you don't have the time to develop a customized list of followers, awareness campaigns are ideal. They are great for getting exposure quickly and determining who is engaging with your followers most cost-effective, fastest method via Twitter.

Tweet Engagements - Although they have less reach than the awareness campaign type, Tweet Engagements concentrate more on actual responses and clicks, likes and likes. This is a better option than Awareness when you're working with a limited budget and know precisely the people you're looking to reach.

Video is the ideal balance between Twitter Engagement and Awareness. Videos have a broad audience and allow the user to track who is viewing the content. If you're able to create videos, I would suggest at a minimum trying this type of campaign since it could be extremely sticky.

Engagement The Second Strongest Stage of Twitter's Engagement

Engagement is when users begin to connect to your company. You should ask your potential customers to have deeper connections to your business. The most important interactions are comments, retweets and liking a tweet and a follow or someone clicking an image on your post.

What is the importance of engagement Many advertisers do not pay attention to engagement metrics since they're too focused on conversions that they fail to see the value. It's true that engagement is an important indicator of tweet and campaign success. If you can get high engagements from your tweets, it signals to other users the content you've created is of high quality.

It is possible to think of engagement (likes or retweets) by other members as form of democratic validation.

It's a method of having others proclaiming to the world that they are a vouch for your products. If you're able to invest the time and effort to create solid engagement on every tweet you post You'll be more likely to get more click-through rates and ultimately sales than if your tweets are merely zero engagement.

The steps you'll need to follow during the engagement phase are:

1. Find your Key Engagement Find out whether a retweet, a like or follow, or reply or follow is the most significant engagement for your company currently.

2. Highlight the Key Engagement in the tweet copy - If you're really hoping for users to share your tweet, make sure you request it specifically in the tweet copy. They're more likely to take the action you're aiming for by stating it clearly in the tweet's copy.

3. Pay attention to Replies and Be Careful People are typically extremely loud on Twitter. Be sure to read responses to your tweets, especially those that aim to drive engagement. People can say things that are offensive and even if you're not there defend yourself, it could influence how others perceive your posts. The same way do not get into a heated debate on Twitter be sensible and focused when you respond to comments Anger is not an appropriate way to conduct yourself!

Engagement is all about beginning conversations therefore the three steps listed above should help you get started. Twitter is an important platform to drive engagement, because of its public format, which allows for an conversations with customers who are about to become. The most effective types of campaigns to correspond to this stage of this funnel would be:

Tweet Engagement - Differently from the Awareness stage, you need to create more meaningful interactions in this stage. The main difference at this point is to follow the steps 2 and 3 mentioned above.

Follower - A follow works similar to sending an email on Twitter. All of your content is sent to all of your customers 100% of the time. This means that you are given the freedom to communicate as often or as little as you like. Follow is a long-term engagement that I recommend as a method of creating continuous brand engagement.

Website Visits If you're using site visits to boost engagement, you should consider adding an pixel for conversion tracking in the page that you direct visitors to. The reason for this is that even if the purpose of this should be an engagement strategy, you shouldn't expect your users to do much on the website initially. If you do put an pixel in the page you can track the visitors' information and then retarget them with conversion-related campaigns.

Examination (Long-term Engagement)

In this phase of the funnel, you'll need users to interact with longer-length content. Potential customers can sign to receive email newsletters download white papers or begin free trials for instance. The content can be longer and more comprehensive as compared to before.

For the record, considering isn't an area in which Twitter excels as a social media platform. Engagement and Awareness come more naturally on the platform. The running of campaigns can remain successful, however the amount of work needed is a bit more than the initial two phases.

The importance of consideration - If your service or product is priced at a the highest price it isn't easy to persuade someone to purchase your product, even with brand recognition, high engagement, and a great landing page. To generate demand and interest to purchase your item, offering free information, insight or a trial copy of the product you offer is an effective method of testing. Take a look at Spotify. They make use of a freemium model to get users to the front door and hopefully turn them into paying customers later. When you've enrolled in the service, you're less likely to purchase another's product.

The steps for nailing Consideration are as follows:

1. It is important to clearly define what causes the user to make a purchase It is essential to present the most persuasive information you can to the reader at this point. If, for instance, I want to get a reader to buy my book and I want to understand the factors that will motivate the reader to purchase it. In this instance I could mention the possibility of earning a profit from ad spending that comes with purchasing my book because I'm aware it's crucial to marketers.

2. Separate the Content into multiple formats - A landing page, one video , or one tweet and image combination won't help you get there. You'll need to test a

variety of formats of conversion, so ensure you have that powerful piece of information in tweets, blogs infographics or videos, etc. to use for your advertisements.

3. Graphics, numbers, quotes or numbers

If I'm trying to make my ebook more popular and tell marketers that I'll make them money doesn't do the trick any more. Informing them about the amount I'll spare them. A quote from an expert, cutting-edge research or an impressive review gives credibility. Images or graphic content is the perfect way to break down complicated ideas into digestible tweets. It's important to remember that simply telling what you want to say won't be as persuasive than expressing what you wish to convey.

There are actually two kinds of campaign types that work:

Video - As opposed to the engagement campaign, you'll need to focus your video towards that crucial aspect I mentioned prior to. For instance, instead of discussing the content of my book I'd make a video that talks about the ROI of the advertising spend and why it's important.

Website visits Follow the above steps of including different formats you can drive traffic to. If you are selling a product, a YouTube page is perfectly fine. If you've got a landing site, it's great, but remember to highlight numbers or Quotes, as well as Graphics. If you have an exact quantity or keyword in the advertisement I suggest mentioning it on your landing page too. The conversion rate is higher for people who have they have a consistent experience.

Conversion

Not last is the conversion phase. This is the point where Twitter is struggling when compared to its rivals. Facebook as well as Google are two of the platforms that excel in Direct Response (DR) advertising which is advertisements that are focused on converting. It doesn't mean that Twitter isn't able to drive conversions; however, it's not going to perform as well as it might have for users with Google and Facebook.

What is the importance of conversion? do not think it is necessary to discuss the reasons why a stage that is focused on conversion is essential, but I'll say it's crucial to separate it in your campaigns from other stages. The intense focus on optimizing of cost-per-click, click rate , and conversion rate could cross paths with something that resembles tweets that have very high levels of engagement. Therefore, to prevent your optimizations from attempting to achieve two goals, I would suggest keeping your campaigns distinct.

The steps needed to convert on Twitter change frequently, but it boils to two essentials:

1. Always keep optimizing A/B tests Content refreshes, changing the targeting, shifting the bid or suspending and then resuming your campaigns. Whatever you're doing, optimizing your campaign is crucial to drive results on Twitter. I've not seen any campaign show reoccurring DR results for more than a week one time. If the campaign isn't working after 36-48

hours , or approximately $1000 spent (whichever is first) then it's time to change the direction and test something different.

2. Start Big Ideally I would advise my advertisers to start by launching multiple campaigns. A separate campaign is for every target audience, type, and bid. That means that If you have 3 types of targeting and 2 distinct audience types, you will start with six campaigns. This method of starting with broad allows you to swiftly determine the campaign (targeting creative, bid combination) is most effective for your needs.

3. Refine - After the campaigns have been running for 24 to 36 hours, you should begin getting a clear view of the direction. Re-evaluate each campaign and suspend the ones that aren't performing well. Then, take the budgets from these campaigns and place it into the most successful campaigns.

4. Optimize - I mentioned in step 1 that you must always be optimizing , but I've added it to step 4, too, because it's just as important. Even after you've discovered

some effective campaigns, you need to check them regularly (every every day) to alter your target audience and the creative.

This is a numbers-based game, and measurement is the key. Conversion tracking should be set up (how to do this is in Chapter 6) and two kinds of campaigns that are almost entirely.

Visitors to your website and conversions In this phase it's crucial to have conversion tracking set up so that you can measure the actual outcomes for your campaigns. In the event that you're running an Web Visitors and Conversions campaign that is not tracking conversions it's as if you're shooting blind. You must ensure that the tracking is in place and work towards your primary goal of conversion.

Mobile App Installs - Created specifically for advertisers of apps The MAP campaigns are designed to drive users to either Google Play Store or the App Store as well as to the Google Play store. In either case, the steps above are equally effective in this kind of campaign.

The goal is to find to find the optimal balance of costs per conversion and quantity. Although there's no one method to convert people at the end of the funnel There are many data points that you can draw upon to help you refine your strategies in this phase. I go deeper deep into my dashboards in chapter 8 about Optimizing.

Chapter 3: Breaking Down The Types Of Campaign

I've just gone through the funnel of marketing and the best way to arrange your Twitter campaigns within that funnel. If you don't have funnels, I'll discuss the strengths and weaknesses of each type of campaign in the following chapter.

According to this guide, Twitter has 5 campaign types. The types of campaigns are awareness, tweet engagements Followers, Promoted Videos and Website Clicks or Conversions and Re-Engagements or App Installs. Each type of campaign comes with an entirely different billing system and optimization algorithms. In this section I'll go over not just their strengths, but also the weaknesses type, but also their billing strategy and how Twitter assesses the success of each type of campaign and my top tips for each.

Awareness Campaigns
The most organic types of campaigns to have appeared through Twitter in recent times, this one is been tailored to Twitter's

strengths the brand's recognition. It gives you a broad reachquickly and at a low cost. It's certainly not suitable for people seeking the most engagement or conversions however. The goal of awareness is to get the maximum amount of attention to an article as is possible.

Billing - Charge per 1000 impressions delivered. It doesn't matter whether you had 1000 clicks or zero however, you'll be charged regardless of whether the impressions are sent.

Optimization The algorithm is going to focus on a important aspect here. What "targeted is your target audience"? I.e. Are you able to reach a wide audience as everyone who follows Beyonce, Ellen Degeneres and Barack Obama? Or is it more specific , like "Social media influencers"? An audience that is broad doesn't always produce excellent results. Twitter tends to reward specific audiences with higher outcomes.

Strengths - Driving massive exposure to a set of tweets or one tweet. Giving the best exposure. This is ideal for announcements in press, brand updates or for locating audiences.

The weaknesses are that it can hinder the engagement of users or converting them. This shouldn't be used to drive users to your site in the hope of gaining Retweets or to collect emails.

Campaigns for Tweet Engagements

The primary ingredient of Twitter Engagements via Tweets, or ads are the longest-running campaign type available on the platform. As I said before it's focused on getting users to engage, click or comment, follow or follow your tweet.

The cost of billing - Each engagement is an expense. That means that any action will count as an engagement. Engagements include clicks, likes, retweets, clicks or replies. The cost is referred to as the cost for each engagement. The impression or views of the tweet aren't considered to be an engagement.

Optimization - The most important measure of success in this case is the Engagement Rate. Engagement rate is an amount of interactions multiplied in the amount of views. The higher the number, the higher Twitter will provide you with lower-cost engagements as well as higher amounts of engagements. All optimizations should be carried out to increase the number of engagements in this kind of campaign.

Benchmarks - The majority of campaigns have a range of 1-3 percent engagement rate. The 1% mark is generally considered to be low, while the mark of 3% should be considered to be high. Cost per engagement is usually within the $1-3 range. I'd be very cautious that my engagements are costing significantly more than $1, since I believe that the value of engagement doesn't actually amount to $3 unless you sell items that cost more than $1,000.

Strengths: Relatively low cost per engagement when compared to the value you receive. Engagement is a great tool to initiate a dialogue with your clients.

Its weaknesses are not ideal to build an database of emails or for driving purchases. The type of campaign used does not do well in removing people from Twitter.

Followers

Followers are the second-oldest type of campaign on Twitter in my experience. aware. It's a kind of campaign that is focused on branding. The primary objective for Followers is expand the number of followers you have. It's an investment that will last for a long time. I would recommend this to businesses that are committed to organic engagement. This is particularly beneficial for companies with lengthy time to convert such as Software Sale or car or Real Estate purchase.

Billing - Per Follower acquired. If someone follows you, but removes themselves from your account and you don't get charged, it won't cost them anything. This is a major concern for many advertisers, but there's nothing to be concerned about. I'm not certain of the exact period of time since companies don't give you such information, however it was quite generous from my experience.

Optimization - The higher follow rate the better your campaign will perform. Follow rate is simply multiplied by the number of impressions. A high rate of follow can result in lower costs per follow, and the reverse is also true. When optimizing, focus on the most popular types of targeting that have the highest follow rate and eliminate everything else.

Benchmarks - The majority of campaigns have the .1-.3 percentage follow rate - far less than the engagement rates. However the majority of advertising agencies I've dealt with were able to offer the $1.50 or $4.00 expense per following. Some might think, "Whoa, that's super expensive!" I'd agree, it's.

One thing to keep in mind is that loyal followers and unfiltered, which means that your content will be sent to all of your followers all the time. This isn't the case with Facebook. Consider that it's an investment that will last for a long time and buying a new follower today could result in a purchase in the future , as well as a voice for your company on Twitter.

Strengths - Email is one of the most beneficial ways to engage online today is engagement via email. One of the things that could be considered to be stronger is an email sign-up and it can cost a lot more. The downsides - It's a lengthy term investment , and if you don't have organic followers, it could be a serious cash-sucker. If you don't make use of the service, they will eventually stop following you , or you don't consider the benefits that they bring to your business.

Promoted Video Campaigns

The platform isn't accessible to everyone. this platform, videos advertisements are a little more complex tool than Tweet Engagements followers or awareness. Videos can often generate tons of impressions within very short time, and have some pretty impressive viewing rates.

Billing There are two methods to be invoiced during a campaign to increase views on your video. The first is to bill when your video is 100 percent in view for the full duration of three seconds. This is a very excellent standard to be able to meet for any video,, so it will limit the amount of views that you can get from your campaign. The other option is that you will be billed for when the video is 100 percent in view for two seconds, with autoplay turned activated. I would recommend using the second option since autoplay is pretty much used today, so it seems more natural. However, some believe that making users click "play" implies that there is an inclination to view.

Optimization - No matter how you setup for billing Twitter examines the view rate or impressions divided by views. When you set a timer of 3 seconds 100% view default, it will typically lower your view rates and increase the price per click. With a two-second auto play, you is almost certain to have higher views, but at an affordable cost. I am convinced that Twitter optimized for views regardless of the billing type, so the second type of billing will probably yield higher returns at the final.

Benchmarks - I have seen views ranging from just 5 percent up to 50% so there's no standard. If you've got something in the region of 15% view rates I'd say that's to be a decent campaign, and expect to have a cost per click that is in the tens of dollars to tens of cents. If your view rates are extremely low, like one-five percent, you could have to pay more than $1 for each view.

Strengths - Video ads have the highest view rate of any kind on Twitter. I've seen companies receive up to 50% views. This is one in two people stopping to look at the video in some manner. This is an incredible amount of involvement for any marketing campaign.

The weaknesses - High views do not always translate into higher click-through rates. My most consistent direct response clients rarely use video due to its extremely low, if not zero conversion rate.

Campaigns for Conversions or Website Clicks

This type of campaign is the most popular direct response method of advertising on

Twitter (for non-app-based advertisers that is). If you're trying to bring users to a website or landing page, particularly in the hopes of getting them to sign to download, sign up for or buy something Campaigns for Website Click are the best option.

Billing The billing option is Twitter has recently changed to a single billing option and that's on a cost per basis. Pay when somebody clicks on the hyperlink in your advertisement. It's that simple.

Optimization - Like other forms of campaigns in this instance, it's all about the frequency with which you earn clicked divided by amount of impressions that are delivered. This is also known as"Click Rate (CR). The more you increase your rate, the more likely Twitter will get lower Cost Per Click (CPCs). This is how the system is optimized, but I'd manually optimize to increase conversion rates, too. This information is stored at the tweet and target level, so you are able to easily determine where you're getting not only the highest rate of clicks but also the most amount of purchase, for example.

Benchmarks - This differs by industry, but the majority of users fall within the band of .1-.3 percentage click rates. This is approximately $1-4 for each click. According to my experience it's difficult to say what you can do to alter costs per click in the first place. This is heavily dependent on the audience that you're trying to reach. The click rate could be something that you control quite a bit about and makes an enormous impact. If you are noticing that you're getting below the .1 percent click rate, make sure you mix the content of the tweet along with the creative and the targeting in the same order. Whatever you do in order to boost the number up will help to revive your marketing campaign. It will also help to keep it running.

Strengths - Through the mix of optimization on a regular basis and the use of Twitter's tracking tools, converting is possible through Twitter via this type of campaign.

Insufficiencies - The truth is that Twitter frequently falls short of its peers like Facebook and Google in generating conversions on the same cost or scale. In the majority of cases, when that scale is achieved or the cost is met typically, it requires more effort than other platforms.

App Installations and Re-Enrollments

This type of campaign performs similar to Conversions or Website Clicks, however with some minor distinctions.

Payment - You can choose to pay per click on an app or per app installation. Pay per click on apps generates more clicks, and in general higher volumes of results. Pay per installation is, however is more manageable and can sometimes be for a half lower cost. However, when I tried this pricing method with advertisers, I'd typically observe the delivery of ads (impressions delivered) decrease to as much as one-tenth of the amount it was prior to. If you had 1000 ads yesterday and you only got 100 today. This is a major issue when you're trying to generate the results that can be scaled.

Optimization - Just like Conversions or Website clicks the algorithm optimizes the amount of money. If you choose to pay the app's click rate per application, Twitter will look to determine how many people clicked and how many impressions generated. If you've put per app installation and you'll see that it examines the frequency of people installing your application.

Benchmarks - The same warnings as the other types, but this will vary according to industry. But, you should be within the area between $0.50 cost per app click , and an .2 to .3 percent app click rate. Cost per install, which is similar to the cost of conversion is different from advertisers to advertisers.

Strengths strengths Twitter is said to be a mobile-first company. While there, we observed about 70% of users who were mobile, so most likely the majority. This makes it an ideal platform to drive app downloads. In addition, Twitter owns MoPub, an ad-exchange for mobile apps that can scale over Twitter by itself.

The weaknesses - Similar to the campaign to convert websites Cost and scale can typically be achieved more easily with other social media platforms. Cost per installation is typically higher for Twitter than Facebook. Twitter in comparison to Facebook specifically.

Section 2 Application of Best Practices

Chapter 4: Targeting & Building Your Audience

One of the first steps you'll have to think about when putting together your marketing funnel is to create the target for your followers on Twitter. In this article I'll go over the details on the different methods you can target Twitter and also what the best methods are for each kind.

Before I breakdown them There's a crucial difference to be made between the two methods to reach out on Twitter. The first group of filters for targeting is subtractive, that is, they eliminate individuals from the overall size. If you use a location or gender filter, for instance the pool will shrink but not larger. The other kind of filtering for targeting is adding people to the total audience size. For example, if adding a username in your targeted audience and then include a keyword then the system will focus on users across both of the segments.

General Best Practices

As a general rule I prefer to stay clear of more than required subtractive filtering for targeting. Devices and location are the two that I normally use. According to my experience, gender Age, Language, and Gender do not apply to all advertisers. If you do are in a niche market, like alcohol sales then age-targeting like age-targeting, for instance is required.

Locating Targeting (Subtractive)

Like the name implies that way, location targeting restricts ads' delivery to certain cities, states/provinces or countries and even ZIP codes. At the time of writing, Twitter has targeting open to virtually all countries around the globe except for a handful of. Certain countries, including those of the US, Canada and UK even have zip codes or provincial level targeting.

My primary recommendation is to do not target more than one country simultaneously.

It is possible to limit the language you use to "English only" however the method you use to create the tweet content for Spain isn't the same to the way you create tweet copy for the US. This is the reason I suggest splitting location targeting according to the language spoken in the country you are targeting, in case there are different languages spoken in the first place apart from English for the nations you want to target.

Age and Gender Aiming (Subtractive)

Twitter has gender and age-based targeting, but , truthfully it never felt as accurate to me. I'm not an engineer, so I cannot really speak about the accuracy however in my experience, both age and gender targeting didn't seem to meet their objectives when I used through them with advertisers. This is a more fundamental issue due to the privacy that the site provides.

In contrast to Facebook, Twitter opted not to gather gender or age data for anyone at the start, which is why I suggest staying clear of these data except when absolutely required.

If you're an alcohol-related brand for instance, you have to apply 21+ targeting . Additionally, if you're an all male site or all women's it is also possible to restrict gender-based targeting. I wouldn't bet on it to be 100% accurate. Instead it's more accurate in the direction of.

Language (Subtractive)

The language targeting format is by far the most straightforward target format. In essence, each user can choose to set their Twitter to appear in the they would like to speak. Thus, whatever you select as the language you want to target, Twitter just delivers the advertisement to those with their Twitter set to the language of that. For my European advertisers, one thing to keep in mind is that certain countries are naturally bilingual. A good instance could be the Netherlands. The country's native language is Dutch but, in particular, in the fields of marketing and business most people also use English. Even though they are able to speak English well, a lot of them have the majority of their Twitter account in Dutch as it's their first language. So, you're secure in focusing on English or Dutch natives (no requirement to limit your search to the English language only) in countries with this type of language. On the other hand the other hand, if you're targeting only Spanish speakers to be in the US there are many bilinguals who are actually setting their accounts for English rather than Spanish. I suggest limiting to Spanish first , and then see whether the reach is too small. You can then try other targeting options if audience isn't reaching.

Platforms, Devices as well as Carriers (Subtractive)

The platform, device and carrier filters let you to limit the display of ads depending on the kind of device that users are using Twitter on. It goes one step further, allowing you to target based on what version on the device they use, like the most recent IOS version as well as the most current Android version. The most effective use in this regard is direct reaction marketing. If you are running conversion campaigns on websites limit them only to Desktop as well as Laptop computers can increase conversion rates dramatically. However less people are using Twitter using Desktop and Laptop which means there's a volume limitation.

If you're planning to spend more than $100 per month, you'll encounter this. It is also possible to see an increase in cost per click with that small audience.

Keywords (Additive)

Keywords can be targeted in two primary ways. First, it is what users' bios contain. The second is what they have been tweeting about. For instance, if Lucy Tweets "I cannot wait to buy new sunglasses!" and you're targeting the term "sunglasses", Lucy just joined the people you can target in any campaign using the term. There are some best practices to be followed:

1.) Be Specific "Sunday Blues" could seem like a great idea but it's likely not. Be sure to keep the phrasing and wording precise enough to create a connection between your advertisement and their tweet.

2.) Keyword targeting can be very limited in its reach There aren't as many people are tweeting "I would like to have an extra mattress." Consider phrases that are similar to expand your audience for example "bad nights ' sleep" or "tossing and tossing and."

3.) Choose 50+ keywords for each campaign - Because of the limited potential of a single phrase or keyword, be sure that you give yourself plenty of roads to travel across. I would recommend 50+ however 100+ is typically the most likely to provide the most significant reach.

Followers (Additive)

It's arguably the most efficient and effective method of targeting on Twitter. When you put a username into the "Followers" section of targeting, you're telling, "Please target the followers of this account, as and followers similar to those from this particular account." It is important to note that you're not targeting the account directly. My example is that if your account is Muscle Milk Twitter will not allow you to only choose to target Arnold Schwarzenegger. There are guidelines here to assist you:

1.) Be careful not to Over Target - You're looking to identify a trend within an audience of users. Thus, you should target similar accounts that share an idea. Do you want to reach SMBs? Consider Hubspot, Twitter Small Biz, Hootsuite etc.

2.) The target audience should be between 15 and 25 users - You are able to do less than 15 if a few accounts have huge followings (500,000or more). It is also possible to increase it to 25 if the majority of your handles have very low follower numbers (less than fifty thousand). If your following grows to 10 million or more then you've probably overdone it. Any less than 50,000 isn't enough to bring substantial outcomes.

Interests (Additive)

Twitter states the interest category is created according to what people follow as well as what they tweet and what they are interacting with. In theory this would be a good way to target , but the reality is that the categories of interest are generally general. The use of interest is more like a spray and then pray kind of method. I would suggest using them only to be used in the initial stage of the marketing funnel , and also for campaigns that target general awareness. My two suggestions are to make interest targeting as narrow as is possible and to avoid checking boxes for more than one primary subject matter for each the campaign (such for Automotive or Beauty).

Behavior targeting (Additive)

My experience is that behaviors can be 30 percent more effective than interest however they are still less targeted than follower-targeting. These lists are created by third party (non-Twitter) companies who sell the data to Twitter. Twitter then matches the information to their own user base. Some of them are quite specific, for example "Home valuation of $399,000 or higher". I've got some suggestions to maintain the cleanliness of this home:

1.) Try to limit the number of checked boxes One general category and one sub-category is optimal. For those who are targeting Auto Owners, don't focus on Auto - Loans.

2.) Avoid "Expanding your reach by targeting similar users" In the majority of Cases The reason is that Twitter makes use of this tool to take its best to determine users who share a similar profile like those on these lists. This is counterproductive because the list is already vetted and targeted target audience. The expansion of the list by adding irrelevant details is not what you want to accomplish.

Event-targeting (Additive)

This is pretty self-explanatory at an upper level, but what this does specifically is targeting those who are engaged in tweets and tweeting about or following tweets related to an event in particular. For instance the 2017 MLB Draft. MLB Draft builds a list of people who are engaging with this kind of content on Twitter.

1.) Similar to before Make it Specific Don't try to target every sporting occasion in there. Pick a few and then tailor your tweet's content to that event to make sure the user understands how to respond.

2.) Add this targeting I would not just focus on the event targeting. I also would focus on key people, speakers or businesses at an event. This offers more options than the basic targeting options

Twitter offers, which could aid in reducing the cost of a bid.

Television Targeting (Additive)

It's pretty distinctive to Twitter TV targeting is an excellent tool , especially if you're advertising on TV at a particular time. The best part is that even if you don't have the money to buy TV ads This is a good alternative. It provides to reach the same people that a large network does for less cost. Similar to television targeting, event targeting targets people who are engaging by specific programming for specific shows.

1.) Limit the tweet to one or two Shows. Ideally, they should be closely linked and the tweet's copy should be specifically for the TV show(s) you're targeting.

2.) Layer on top of real TV Ads - If are able to afford this is a fantastic method of getting attention from a potential viewer after they've seen your advertisement on TV.

Targeted audiences (Additive or Subtractive)

The majority of the other types of targeting are determined by Twitter it is the only kind of targeting that allows you to create the audience from the bottom from the ground. Tailored audiences are designed by two methods. One option is to upload an account of your users (emails, Twitter id's etc) and then Twitter matches it to active, verified users. Another option is to design an ad-hoc conversion tracking pixel and let that pixel gather data about users from the place you put the pixel to. If you've established a large enough audience (1000plus active users) You'll be capable of adding or subtracting this list of audience members from the targeting of any campaign. There are some best methods to follow here:

1.) A personal list is ideal if you have a pre-existing audience and you're looking for innovative methods to target and connect with them. The other side is that the match-rate of Twitter (the amount of emails per the number of users your audience actually corresponds with) has historically been low. I would suggest at least 10,000 email addresses before creating a Twitter-based audience by using the help of an email database.

2.) Making use of lists created from Pixels is the simplest solution for the majority of advertisers. The most efficient use-case is the retargeting. Imagine that you've spent long hours moving customers from awareness to consideration through the funnel, and they have visited your website but haven't purchased any products. Making a specific campaign to the users who is targeted in the text of tweets and is focused on those that have visited the website but not bought anything is an important method to get them to the purchase.

3.) Eliminating Users is a Good Idea to avoid targeting the already converted user Imagine someone who has bought previously so you would not like them continue to receive the ads. Simply go to "Limit Audience by excluding targeted audiences" and choose that group of buyers. Twitter will make sure they don't receive any advertisements that are delivered to them.

Chapter 5: Twitter And Creative Copy

If there's a component of an Twitter campaign that's more important than the targeting, it's creative. Although I do have good guidelines I've also learned that you must look into and try out. Bidding, Targeting, etc. are the main components of constructing the perfect Twitter campaign, while creativity and copywriting can be described as the arts. In this section I'll provide a brief explanation about the various kinds of creatives as well as provide tips particular to every.

Tweet Copy

Think that this is the main point of your advert. If it is not cooked properly it may create a bad impression in the mouth of a potential buyer. The Tweet Copy is content that you write into your tweet. Although you are able to include text in an image or as the form of a headline, I do not think that these are as effective as the standard 140-character count tweet you compose for every advertisement. If you do it right it can dramatically boost click rates on your tweet. Here are some tips to remember:

1.) Make it as clean as you can The more information you add to your tweets the less effective they are at driving a single click. If you're looking to generate clicks for websites make sure you don't use #'sor @'s. Make sure to limit the tweets to one single link. If you're hoping to get replies, do not include any other information. Simply announce that you'd like to reply on the tweet. Do not offer users any other method to interact with them other than the one engagement that you're trying to achieve.

2.) Connect the Copy to the content on your website Remember that among the most important factors that affects conversions of users is the consistency. If your tweet boasts 15% off, but your website is selling for 10%, visitors will notice. And even more so when you're talking about an important aspect in your tweets, like battery life, but this feature isn't mentioned on your landing page, it can make users confused. Be sure to keep your content consistent when the user moves the tweets to reach your landing pages.

3.) Test, Test and Test Again Test, Test and Test Again - It's very likely that the first three concepts for tweet copy won't be the best. To make it easier, ensure that you're always trying out new content. I recommend that at the very least every one to two weeks you revisit your campaigns and revise the copy of your tweets. Start by looking at your top-performing Tweets . Then, model two new tweets based on the most effective tweet copy and add them to your campaign. Switch off any other tweets that are not performing at that point.

Tweet Creative

When I say creative, I'm referring to any media content, such as videos or images. There are two major types of formats you can choose to use for your creative purposes in any tweet such as card and other non-card formats.

Cards

Cards are basically images or video that has pre-defined specifications and an image or video that is embedded within the image. The principal goal of cards is to ensure that tweets are clean and free of any clickable content that I told you about previously. There are three kinds of cards that are available on Twitter Ads at the moment.

Website Cards - Created to increase conversions and clicks on websites campaigns, websites cards simply insert the link to the site you wish the user to visit inside a photograph. The card is also adorned with the headline and brief description beneath the image.

1.) The first requirement for success is to ensure that the image meets the specifications of the card for your website. If the image you are using has been cut or is is too large in some way , it could be a problem for the card on your website this could cause viewers to hit the image trying to expand it only to be directed to your site. The majority of people who visit an unintentionally visited website don't stay. It is a waste of your money.

2.) The second step is to ensure that the headline and call-to-action match the tweet. Some prefer to copy text from tweets for headlines and calls to action. Personally, I like keeping the two elements similar, but not exactly identical. A short, concise and ideal 3 words or less work the most effectively.

Images App Card – Used for the App Installs campaign type This is the same technique as the web card. However, instead of driving users to an online site, it connects via Google Play Store or the App Store, or Google Play Store. It is also possible to use this type of card to encourage re-engagement for your app, when it's installed on the user's smartphone.

1.) Examine different image types. Lifestyle and graphic images are the two most effective types. Try both. Based on my experience, graphic images work best in game applications and lifestyle images work well for applications for business or utility.

2.) Create a headline and tweet copy to match your landing page on the app store. Make sure that the information you include in your text is repeated within the application store. If you're using a graphic image and want to include it on the page for the app store is an excellent way to increase the conversion rate.

Video App Card : This kind of card is slightly different from an image card as it uses videos in place of static images inside the tweet. I must say that my clients had mixed results using this format. Some noticed huge improvement over static images while others were flat.

1.) Make sure that the video is short.15 second or less will give you the best viewing speeds.

2.) Use flashy images. People love bright colours and swiftly moving images. The bright and flashy look is the most effective method to convince someone to get off their screens and click.

Non-Card Creative

You have two options Images and videos. When you write organic tweets, you may also make use of gifs however, as of writing, gifs are not supported by advertisements.

Video - The need for video is fairly straightforward. As I said earlier the length of video is crucial. Take into consideration the user's point of from a different point of view. The majority of users use their phones in the field (LTE 4G, LTE, etc.) and often commute or using public spaces. This means that quick, fast videos are often more effective than longer-form ones.

1.) Limit it to 30 seconds - My experience has been that I have seen videos with under 30 seconds or close to 15 seconds were the most effectively. Remember the last moment you were required to view an advertisement for a 30-second video on YouTube. The less time you spend, the more effective.

2.) You might want to consider adding subtitles The majority of users don't wear headphones and turning up the volume is generally considered inappropriate in public spaces. If you've got subtitles, I've noticed that you can get engaged with a number of people who would otherwise been scrolling.

Pictures - At this stage, it's likely that you have a good idea of the kinds of images that perform well and what don't well on Twitter However, there are some other considerations to make.

1.) Images are a lot more flexible than cards - You are free to experiment with sizes and formats. Be aware that if your image is too big it could split both sides of the timeline of the user, making it look a bit sloppy.

2.) Avoid text on images In actual fact, Facebook has a specific ratio wherein images can't contain more than 30 percent text since it can affect performance. In this situation I suggest not having more than 3 words per image. Ideally, you should not have any text on any image. That's what the tweet's copy is there for!

3.) Bright and flashy get users to stop scrolling - Similar to videos, bright colors grab the attention and stop people from scrolling. I suggest including at minimum two bright colors, such as red, yellow or pink in your images to increase engagement.

The art of tweet writing and design isn't easy for anyone people who aren't naturally creative. It's an unnatural art form that is difficult to master. My experience has taught me that that while there is a ideal image, or the perfect tweet copy , doesn't exist. Instead, a consistent test schedule and a small investments in top-quality images can help a lot. Use the top practices mentioned above and you'll discover the combination that will benefit your company within a matter of minutes! In the next section I'll discuss more of the math that goes into the creation of your campaigns.

Chapter 6: Budgeting, Bidding, And Conversion Tracking

I've tied these three topics in order to highlight their technical nature. I'll begin by discussing my top practices to set and manage budgets. I'll then go over the different types of bidding and the best ways to make the most of each. I'll also go over how to set up tracking of conversions and the reasons it is important for you.

Setting Budget

You may already have a budget by your personal financials. If so it is best to leave this section out. If you're not sure, here's a couple of ways to set the amount you budget for on Twitter. The first step is to revisit your goals. How many conversions require to occur in order to support your company in a meaningful manner? By "conversions," I refer to any metric that is important to you: purchase or sign-ups, responses, and so on. Once you have that number in your mind, just apply the double-cost rule to the number. Example: If 100 sign-ups will make a significant difference to your business, and we are aware that each sign-up costs around 20 dollars, then I'd multiply that number to 40 and then multiply that by 100. Therefore, your budget will be 4000 dollars. The reason I'm doubling the amount is because you'll get very little attention initially, but very significant progress towards the end your campaign. This is because the majority of people learn to maximize and narrow their tweets and targeting on the most successful users but this is usually only the middle of their campaign.

The majority of people learn to improve and narrow their tweets and their targets on the most effective users, but this is usually not until the middle of their campaign.

Another method to establish an amount for budgeting is declare "how much money can I afford to invest?" While this is an individual choice I've got some quick questions to aid you in your quest. First, how much will you be able to spend without getting any results but still be able to do so from a cash flow perspective? In the second, how much has been spent on other marketing techniques during the past month, and what amount are you willing to reduce this to make room for Twitter? Thirdly, how much have you set aside to investing in your business every month?

Bidding

Bidding, unlike budgets, is designed to reduce the costs of engagements and interactions on Twitter in comparison to the overall cost. While budget can be thought of as your energy usage total however bidding can be thought of like the efficiency of how you make use of the energy. Twitter offers a variety of methods you can bid on, each having specific applications.

Automated - By far the most simple option, automated bidding is simply putting bidding in the hands of the computer. Twitter will then do its best to strike a balance between costs and reach. Based on my experience, automated bidding tends to favor reaching over cost. This means that if you're trying to stretch your budget, then automatic bidding is a great option. It will definitely assist you in doing this. If you're trying for the lowest price per transaction I'd suggest one of the bidding methods.

Target Cost Target Cost is a similar offer to Facebook or Google You may have heard of Target bidding. If you are, feel free to bypass this section. Setting a goal cost informs Twitter that you've set an objective spend per transaction, but that within reason that you're willing to spend a bit more than or below that amount. The goal of Twitter isn't to get you to that exact cost in the first or the second day. The aim is to spread out costs over a period of time so that it is close to the amount you want to spend. One reason why this method is superior to the Maximum Bid (an old type of bidding that Twitter had) is because the costs for interactions fluctuate throughout the day. While you don't wish to spend more than 5 dollars per click for your advertising campaign, users' activity could be extremely high at 6:35 pm , with more conversion rates, too. The cost will go up in line with the value of customers and the demand. Twitter will then decide to spend a little more in order to gain the most valuable users. In order to make up the price, Twitter will then be more affordable in other time of the day when the value is less and it isn't necessary to bid as much to get a click. This is the best method of bidding in any type of performance-based advertising , and I would highly recommend it to conversion-focused advertisers.

Bidding can be a bit complicated however at the end of every day there's only one important guideline to follow. If your aim is to increase to increase awareness and reach, then utilize automated bidding. If you are looking for the conversion of results it is recommended to use targeted bidding.

Conversion Tracking

Be prepared because we're about to be a little technical. I'll explain the concept of conversion tracking and how it functions, and then how you can use it to create Twitter ads. It's a standard technology, so it's not unfamiliar to you. If so it is, this article should clarify what this technology does and the way it operates.

How do you define Conversion Tracking?

In the simplest of sense, conversion tracking is an online site's method of tracking users as they move through the internet. When the user is on the conversion page that you connected to in your campaign the pixel that tracks conversions informs Twitter. Twitter will then record that information the conversion page and adds it to your campaign. The conversion page could be a thank-you page that is displayed after someone has made purchases or sign-up for your service. Conversion tracking comes in a few names. I usually see"Conversion Tracking" Pixel or Web Pixel.

What exactly is a "pixel"? What is it?

Great question. If you've purchased a TV within the last 10 years, then you've been familiar with the word "resolution" as well as other trendy terms such as HD and Ultra HD. These are all measurements of the number of pixels in a square. In essence what is the smallest square of color could I squeeze in one square inch?

A pixel is a small square that appears on the display of your computer or web page. It's the same with your personal computer, and even websites! Websites comprise thousands of pixels side to side, which make up one color, slowly forming the numerous videos, images and other content that are available online.

What is happening with Twitter, Facebook and the entire advertising industry do is take the pixel in the webpage (usually toward higher up) to replace the original one with a ding-pixel which has a piece of code in it. If a user goes to the webpage on your website where the pixel is storedon, the pixel will be loaded and the tiny line of code is sent through Twitter to inform it "Hey this is so and that has been to the page you mentioned is an essential page!" and records it for the campaign. Based on the pixels you place on what page, it reports the type of conversion back to Twitter.

The Types of Conversion Pixels available on Twitter

There are various kinds, and you can find them under the "Tools and Conversion Tracking" section of the dashboard. The pixels can be used to track any of the following: the purchase, a site visit or Download, as well as Sign Up as well as "Custom". It is true that, for the most part every type performs exactly the identical thing. The labeling of the tab with the type is an easy way of tracking the specific pixel's doing in the next section of the dashboard. As an example when I label my pixel's site visit, I will put it on my home page , and examine the results of my campaign, whenever someone who is engaged by my campaign is directed to my home page, it is recorded as the visit. You can also identify this pixel as an ad hoc purchase pixel however that could cause confusion.

The main difference is the difference between Universal and single Event pixels.

Twitter is actually doing a good job of summarizing this by saying:

A universal tag that converts allows you to apply the tag at a single time and establish rules based on the user's behaviour.

The way they work is that you simply need to put this pixels on your site and it'll be used for recording events from visitors to any page on your site. A single event pixel however is a particular code snippet which will only record events on pages you manually add it. Therefore, instead of creating the pixel one time it is necessary to place it on several pages on your site every time you manually.

Personally, I favor the universal image and would highly recommend it to those who are like me. If you're looking to be able to determine the exact position of the pixel, and don't trust Twitter to make that decision (some users do not!) The single Event Pixel is the best option for you.

Attribution Windows

This causes confusion for a number of advertisers, and I'd like to address this issue quickly. Attribution windows are the window of time in which you're willing to provide Twitter "credit" to the purchase, visit to your site or other activity you track using your pixels. Crediting simply means that you attribute a portion or all of your conversions to Twitter.

You have two options you can award Twitter credit for bringing a user to the conversion pixels.

1.) Post-Engagement attribution - This happens when a person interacts with or clicks on an article in your campaign. The credit period is more flexible in this case since there was a clear intention to connect with your brand or your product in this instance. I typically limit my credit to 15-30 days after clicking. The primary reason I choose to have this long time frame is to determine later whether my campaign had any effect on the purchase of people. Perhaps someone was able to see the advertisement on Twitter but then was able to see it again through Facebook and then looked up the person on Google. The whole process could take a while, but I'd like to acknowledge Twitter for the search, Facebook for the re-engagement and Google to help me locate my product.

2.) Post-View Attribution is simply a way of saying that someone saw your tweet on their timeline, but didn't interact with it or click it. It is important to keep the period of time relatively brief. The most common reason the user might convert even to your site without clicking is when they were on their commute, or some other such thing, and didn't have sufficient information to load your site. When they arrived at work or and they looked for you on the internet. It's not a huge application, but it's still important to track. My suggestion is to keep the view-window to one day.

After we've discussed the technical aspects of Twitter and the best methods for each, we'll move on to benchmarks for campaign performance.

Chapter 7: Benchmarks For Performance Of Campaigns

The key metrics of every campaign are based on averages. These can assist you in making a decision about how your campaign is doing. These benchmarks, or averages, are separated into two factors: campaign type and industry. Before I present the benchmarks, let me clarify that these guidelines are built on own experience and will change over time. The benchmark I choose for an actual benchmark for click rates today could be different than the benchmark of click rate within two years. Utilize these benchmarks as the basis to determine your campaign rates and averages.

Follow Rate of .1-.3 The range is pretty typical. If you're seeing less than .1 percent, I'd certainly alter the target. Anything above .3 percent is excellent and you'll probably have your cost per follow decrease due to this.

Cost per Follow: $2-$4 per follow. It varies widely depending on the industry, so B2B for example usually pays close to $4, and occasionally more than five dollars per following. Consumer facing or B2C may generally get close to $2. Entertainment is the sector with the lowest prices according to my experience, around $1-$2 per follow.

Engagement Rate - between 1 to 3 percent is the norm. It's not uncommon for properly designed campaign to reach an engagement rate of 3% or more. rate, so it's still normal to have 1% when your campaign falls below 2percent, I'd suggest changing the copy, creative or the targeting.

Cost per engagement - It ranges widely, but from my experience that it is around $1 for each engagement is pretty common. Although I've seen some companies who pay more than three dollars for each event in the B2B market I don't think it's a good idea. Engagements don't provide enough value to warrant greater than one dollar. If I had my own money, I'd want to increase that amount to the $.50 mark.

Click Rate - Similar to the Follow Rate figure generally stays low. Anything in between .2 and .4 percent is considered to be acceptable. Although B2B is more likely to have lower click rates however, it is all dependent on the creative, copy and the targeting. I've witnessed a number of software companies that have achieved more than 1percent click rates for their marketing campaigns. I'd suggest adjusting continuously until you get to a rate close to .5 percent, despite the typical since I'm confident that it's possible with the right approach.

Cost per Click is usually between $1 to $4. "Whoa this is a huge variation!" Yes, it is. I believe that Twitter has an extensive way to go with DR in terms of cost per Click as well as the delivery of those clicks could vary. My general guideline is that I don't think I'll pay less than I'm paying for Facebook but I don't think I'd be able to pay nearly as much as I do for Google. It's somewhere between.

Video View Rates View rates are typically the highest percentage of everything on

Twitter. From my experience, advertisers will stay for anywhere from 10 to 15 percentage. If you're getting more that 15% then you've created a engaging video or tweet. Remember that you can see completion rates for the video, so be watching this.

Cost per View: While rates are quite high however, the price is usually quite low. The cost per viewing should be between $.05 or $.15. If you're getting something more than 15 cents, and you're seeing excellent views (15 %+), it possible that the price quite high for the particular audience. is at a high level right now. If you're typically seeing 15 you'll have a lower cost per view.

The most effective way to utilize benchmarks is to apply them as a guideline for where and how you can improve. Although they are excellent to use, I would not consider them to be a definitive measure of the success of your business. For instance, a large number of clicks doesn't mean that you've succeeded if there aren't any conversions. An impressive engagement rate won't really mean anything if all the engagements you're getting are clicks on the photo in your tweet , but not shares or likes. It's about balancing the goals of the campaign with the outcomes and using benchmarks as a guideline to determine what improvements could be achieved.

The best way to do this is to look at the overall results of the campaign. If something seems to be to be a bit off from the figures above there are three choices.

1.) Optimize the Campaign Examine the data and eliminate the tweets or targeting which have the lowest results. You might want to expand the tweets or targeting which are generating the best results.

2.) Be Reasonable about the Price If you're certain that your target audience is pricey and you're willing to pay the price to get a click, it's completely acceptable. Be sure to check your campaign for any modifications you can implement.

3.) Stop the Campaign If the campaign is so out of date that you can't find any space for improvement It's time to stop the campaign and focus on other campaigns or start another one.

The best practices are essential to managing and optimizing campaigns throughout time. In the next section, we'll go into more advanced techniques on Twitter. This isn't an exhaustive list, but a few of the most popular and useful techniques I came across during my time working at Twitter.

Third Section - Advanced Use Cases & Examples

Chapter 8: The Optimizations

Optimizing is the fundamental base for the more advanced use of Twitter ads. One of the most critical things you can do as an advertiser is always-be-optimizing. There's hardly a point when an advertising program on Twitter is totally dependent on autopilot. Certain Follower campaigns can run for a long time without a single optimization, but , even then you should optimize your campaign at least every few weeks. There are some general rules that I consider to optimize.

1.) First, optimizations are meant to assist, not hurt - so If you're happy with the results of your campaignand they're not slowing down or becoming more expensive do not optimize! There's no reason to fix something that's not broken.

2.) 2. An optimization isn't always the best way to improve the results of a Campaign . Sometimes it may actually hurt the outcome. This is a fact of advertising. While it's an ideal method doesn't mean it's going to work all the time. If the improvement results in less performance, I suggest not doing the work and looking at different options.

3.) Third, if you Are Just Beginning Start by establishing a base long-term campaigns like those that drive followers or conversions will have more results when they include 2-3 variations for each audience and tweets prior to the time of launch. It is possible to optimize campaigns on the fly however, campaigns will acquire high-quality scores over time. This means that a campaign that is not performing well will have a tough time being more successful than a brand new campaign that has no score associated with it. This means that if you've got an idea in regards to what variations you'd like testing on tweets, images, or the targeting of your campaign, you'll want to create separate campaigns from the beginning and then test each variations for their effectiveness. When you've got a method or two that you like then shut down all other campaign and begin improving the best campaigns.

Know where to locate the necessary data to make Improvements

An knowledge of the way that Twitter Ads dashboard works is essential to optimize your campaigns. If you're unsure or don't know what to do but don't worry it's pretty simple. Twitter has invested a ton of time into building out guides on their platform at business.Twitter.com. It is important to study and become familiar with the platform before you start campaigns. It can make a difference in the use of the platform.

The first thing you're searching for is a an overall success rate or failure.

If you look at the campaign-specific data do you find the click or follow rate in line with the benchmarks I mentioned in the previous paragraph? Does the cost per outcome appear to be high or low? Use the benchmarks listed above if do not possess your own. You'll need to pinpoint your problematic campaign(s) as well as your successful campaign(s) frequently and early.

The Twitter Ads dashboard, each campaign can be divided into three fundamental components that are ads (creative) and audiences (targeting) and the history. The majority of the time the audience and ads are where you'll see the most progress in optimizing your performance of the campaign. Likewise, history can help to keep track of the actions you've taken throughout the process.

I'll go over the most important optimizations you can implement for all types of targeted audience and for the most inventive. Utilize these as a starting point to design your own strategies to optimize on Twitter.

Audience Optimization: Usernames

Depending on the method you utilized for targeting, the result of your campaign will be attributable to the strategy that you employed to improve. If you employed follower targeting with 25 handles for instance, your results will be tied to which handles influenced the results for you. When optimizing for handles, you'll need to eliminate the least effective handles. They are those that produce little or no results or with the most expensive cost per outcome. This will reduce your list to 10 pretty quickly. Be sure to keep in mind the delivery. If the amount of advertisements that are being displayed decreases and you'll need to look for new handles that can be added to the campaign. This should be fairly adaptable as username targeting typically is a good size to begin with.

Keywords to Optimize Audiences Keywords

Keywords can be more difficult. This kind of targeting usually has delivery issues for smaller audience. When you're analyzing the results you'll need to include at least one new keyword for each two keywords you remove. Make sure to keep the number of keywords in excess of 50 and , ideally, close to 100, if feasible.

Audience Optimization: Interests & Behaviors

The functions of interests and behaviors are exactly like usernames, however at a larger scale which makes optimization challenging. The most important thing to remember about the interest or behavior is that if broad categories such as Automotive News or Beer are not producing outcomes, I would suggest switching to a username-based targeting and attempting to achieve the same goal using the help of Twitter handles instead. The behavior can be difficult to replace (average earnings of the amount of XXX dollars as an example) however, it's essential to know when the strategy is not performing. Do not let a campaign last longer than a week before you end your losses.

The Audience Optimized: Targeting TV and Event Targeting

In contrast to Usernames or Keywords and Keywords, you're not likely to have much flexibility in deciding which other TV events or shows to target. Most likely, you've compiled several potential match-ups and have only a limited space to work within particularly for occasions. Instead of trying to locate other events or television shows instead, you should focus on the text of your tweet and the creative. If your results aren't being reported or are not showing up, you should make sure whether your tweets use the same language that's in use on a current TV show, or during an event. For instance, if I'm aiming for Techcrunch Disrupt, I'd pay attention to any well-known pitches and include them in my tweets when it's possible. This will make your content more relevant.

Creative Optimizations Tweet Copy

There are two ways to find out whether your tweet's content resonates with the target audience you're aiming. The first is looking at the amount of replies and retweets, or likes. Tweets that have a powerful message that highlights a significant issue for users can often garner many likes, some responses, and perhaps a couple of Retweets. If you're not seeing the likes, it's likely that your message isn't reaching the right people. Another aspect you should examine is the conversion rate after Twitter. What is the number of people actually choose to download, purchase or engage in the last section of your funnel once they've clicked the tweet? If you can answer that with only a few conversions, and numerous clicks, there's a good chance that your tweet doesn't match the content on your site. It's important to get many clicks, however. If you're not seeing clicks, then you shouldn't anticipate a lot of conversions.

To maximize your conversion rate for a single after a post click, you'll need to examine the relationship between what your tweet conveys and the information on your website or landing page is saying. If you're the moms, for instance when your tweet talks about a brand new baby bottle, and the main feature is its ease to clean, and the landing page you're on doesn't mention cleaning, that's the reason you'll see the drop off. Unconformity can appear unprofessional or unprofessional on the web so ensure you've got the same message across all the places you promote the product.

The most important thing to take care of using tweet copy is to ensure to ensure that you don't have too many clickable places. People love being distracted. If you'd like visitors to go to your site but you add an @ handle from another user or an important conversation, you're giving a user a reason to become distracted and to not click your link. Make it easy and limit the amount that is click-able per tweet. If you don't require the click (you're simply promoting awareness) you shouldn't include one!

Creative Optimizations Tweet Creative

I have mentioned a variety of images and cards in my discussion of creative tweet copy and tweets. Although each one may differ slightly but the general rules are identical across all of them.

1.) The creative process is dynamic direction. At any time it is possible to have a great image, but it can only be successful for a specific amount of time. We estimated that somewhere between one to three weeks was the most effective time for single ad. Another way to gauge the efficacy of your current photos are is to use the frequency of your ads as a reference. If you're finding that your ads are being delivered to the same user an average 3 or more times, then I suggest changing the image. This will not only boost the click rate but also provide your advertisement a fresh appearance that is particularly important for advertisers who target smaller audiences.

2.) Try at least two kinds of images. The first one I'd test is a lifestyle picture. It is a picture where people are in "real everyday" situations. A coffee shop patron at their desk is an excellent illustration. You can find them on sites selling stock images for purchase. The other type of image is graphic or image which is predominantly cartoon-based graphic or animated. Imagine an infographic, or anything that needs the use of photoshop or design software to be accomplished. The major drawback here is that graphic images don't typically come from stock-photo websites similar to lifestyle imagery, which means you must pay for it or make it yourself. While graphic images can be slightly more costly and more timely to get due to this, I would still suggest making an effort to put it together because a high-quality graphic image can significantly increase engagement or click rates for an advertising campaign. The two types of images I would suggest experimenting with both on separate tweets within an identical campaign. Examine the results, and decide on the one which is producing the best outcomes for that particular audience.

3.) Beware of distractions from the images. Images can be distracted in various types. The most common form is any type of written or spoken wording that is placed over the image. I'm not sure why most people aren't inclined engaging with images or images that have text on their tops. I'm not sure if it makes them think of billboards, or something else but it's not considered a good idea. In the event that you need to use a logo or the name of a business, etc make sure it is as little and free of obstruction as you can. Do not allow it to be over 25% of the area for image. Additionally the text in an image along with tweet copy and headlines in the case of cards, are an excessive amount of text. Another major distraction is an image that's not suitable for the size of the advertisement. If you're using a particular type of card, it will display the dimensions and require you to cut the image in line with. Beware of cut-offs and awkward angles. I've seen a lot of photos where the top part was abruptly cut off, and nobody clicked since it did not make sense. It's the same for regular tweets. You can have more flexibility with your tweet images however, make sure that your default preview on your timeline (what users are seeing before clicking the advert) will show the entire image, and doesn't cut anything off.

Optimizations are the foundation for the more advanced use of Twitter however there are many other ways to take it to further. In the next section, I'll look at some of the marketing strategies I've discovered to be especially efficient on Twitter.

Chapter 9: Marketing Advanced Strategies

I discussed in chapter 8 the importance of dividing every marketing push in a variety of campaigns that focus on different audiences or tweet combos. The next chapter is going to deconstruct the details of that into a few tactics I've learned from some of my most experienced advertisers throughout the many years.

The first aspect we have to study in depth before diving into strategies is the application of tracking pixels. I did a bit of research on the subject in chapter 6 but this is a crucial tool in generating long-term returns on your advertisements. If you are unsure about the setup or upkeep of the pixel you've chosen, would suggest calling Twitter Help with Ads or an easy Google search. It's an industry standard technology used for advertising.

Leveraging Conversion Tracking

There are several major reasons for using conversion tracking, which makes it a must for marketers.

1.) Tracking results - Conversion tracking, as it's referred to, is designed to assist in recording the number of people who browse, buy or sign up to convert on your site. If you don't have conversion tracking conducting any type of direct response marketing is not responsible. If the only option is to use the campaigns with no the conversion tracking or do not launch the campaigns, then I'd advise against running the ads - it's not important. If users click your ad and visit your site, the pixels are utilized to track every type of conversions. Everything from web page visits, sign-ups downloads, purchases, installs as well as downloads. Be aware of what you're going to track and ensure that the device is monitoring it for you. Once it's been tracked, go through your campaigns regularly to check how many conversions are being generated and for what price.

2.) Building an Audience Many advertisers have a difficult to convert customers starting with the first click of their advertisement. This means that you must be extra careful to accommodate people who have gone through one or two steps through the marketing funnel , but haven't converted fully yet. The most typical scenario is when a person has visited your site but hasn't yet purchased. Conversion tracking pixels lets you to create an audience around these customers to re-target these users with a different campaign. I'll go into more detail about Retargeting in the future. It's important to remember that if you've got an online landing page or website that you could utilize the conversion tracking pixel to create audiences around users of these pages.

3.) Your Site Only - Because conversion tracking pixels need to be installed, it's crucial to remember that you are not allowed to put them elsewhere but on your own website. This is a huge restriction if you're an the internet and sell predominantly via Amazon such as. If tracking your audience and the potential outcomes are vital, my advice is to develop an online landing page that is positioned the middle of Twitter as well as

Amazon. In this way, you can at the very least observe the effect that the ad has in getting customers to your landing page , and start collecting information from those users for future campaigns. It can affect conversion rates in general and it's a case picking the less costly of two options. Another option my friend Lena in the field of digital marketing suggests is to include the Twitter campaign-specific Promo code like "TWTR". This can allow you to in tracking this specific traffic, without having a pixel in the first place.

Marketing Tactic 1 Retargeting

Retargeting or remarketing could be one of the buzzwords that have been trending in digital marketing in the past five years. This isn't something that should be only used on Twitter, but it's a strategy Facebook encourages and something you can try using banner ads too. Retargeting refers to the process of advertising to a person who has already taken an interest in your content, most likely recently. Here's how to get started:

1.) Building an Audience As I said earlier you can create an audience using the conversion tracking pixels. To retargetyour visitors, however, you'll have to go further. You'll need to differentiate users who visit different parts of your site. You'll need a distinct tracker list for each of the following areas of your site.

A) Visitors who've visited the main page of your website

B) Visitors who've visited particular pages of content (blog videos, posts tutorials, blog posts, etc.)

C) Customers of your item to their shopping cart (for online shopping)

D) Users who have bought products or services from you

You can clearly see that every visit serves a distinct reason, so ensure that you have a distinct audience list for every visit. This will help in delivering your ad's content to these people.

2.) Focus on each Audience separately This is the most important thing to do is to match the tweet's creative and copy to the specific action that the user took on your site. If the user has completed several actions (visited the home page as well as the content page) pick the one that is closest to conversion. In this scenario I would pick that page for content. The idea is to point out something that the user may have encountered on the webpage he or visited. Repeating a statistic or quote as an example in your blog article.

3.) Bid higher for lower Funnel Users - By this moment the user has seen your advertisement a few times, and the market in advertising Twitter is often fierce. Being able to get in front for the 4th or 5th time may be difficult from a bidding point of view. My general rule of thumb is that for each stage of the funnel when is nearer than being converted to, you must be prepared to pay between 10 and 20 percent more per click. It's up to you to make your own judgment to determine where you'll be on that scale. The reason is that a person who has nearly converted is going to be more valuable than one who hasn't been to your website, and the amount of users who have converted always be less than the percentage of users who haven't. This means you'll have less opportunities to present your message and thus bid high and placing the correct contents (step 2) to every user is more crucial throughout the process.

4.) Don't forget to include It's not worth showing your advertisement to an existing user without having other products that they would like to buy. Similar to this, when you're targeting users that have already visited your site The pool of users that you will target will also include people that have had a chance to visit content sites or other websites. Make sure you keep these users out of your target audience. Always concentrate on the most distant level of the funnel. I don't think I would want to show the identical "come visit our site" advert to a person who has already visited an article on a particular blog and is clearly deciding to buy.

Retargeting is an expansive strategy that can be a complete book. I strongly suggest that you research other strategies available on the internet in relation to the subject.

Marketing tactic 2: Retargeting Tweet Engager and Video to Direct Response

Twitter is a unique method of retargeting the platform. Tweet Engager Retargeting basically creates an audience from users who are engaged on your Twitter posts. Engagement is the action that a person takes to click expand, retweet/reply or retweet your tweet. There are many methods to make use of this kind of targeting.

1.) Tweet Engager in conjunction with DR Campaigns If you fall into the group of people who send users to a site that does not allow you to track the conversions of their site this also means you can't create an audience for these users. Tweet Engager lets you overcome this hurdle at least in part. If you start an DR campaign, you should think of a website clicks, for example. people will interact with your content , but they may not visit the site which would trigger your conversion pixels. One great strategy is to target these users by sending a different tweet that boasts the value of your offer. This will allow you to continue to engage people who have demonstrated intention but haven't yet decided to go to your site.

2.) Tweet Engager using Brand for DR A different option is to conduct an engagement campaign for brands. Consider tweet engagements. In this way, similar to the DR campaigns mentioned above you create the potential customer base in a affordable way, as compared to driving clicks on your website. Then, you can use this audience to retarget them by launching a click-to-website campaign that drives visitors to your site.

3.) Video to website clicks My most-loved method for the retargeting feature of Tweet Engager is to boost views to a video campaign first. The reason behind this is because videos tend to generate huge numbers of engagements and views for a low cost. After you've created this massive list for a fairly inexpensive cost, you could make them a target for a highly specific web-based visits campaign. It's a cost-effective and efficient way to get people to your website even if just one tweet or other piece of content isn't telling the story enough!

4.) Educational Pushes - If your product is complex and takes a long amounts of explanation, you'll usually be marketing via education. The order in which this content is presented is often crucial too. Targeting your Tweets to engagers is a great method to ensure that you are sending users through an engagement funnel , as opposed to them seeing random tweets that appear at random times. For instance when tweet 1 is read as a result of a search, then for tweet 2I'll aim users who clicked on tweet 1. The campaign that promotes tweet 3 will focus on the people who were engaged via tweet 2, and then on.

Tweet Engager can come to its own when it is incorporated into a bigger marketing strategy. I would highly recommend it to marketers who have a long marketing funnel, complex products or have trouble getting customers to go to their site.

Marketing Tactic 3: Increased Volume advertising using Twitter ads Editor

The secret to unlocking the potential of scale and a cost effective per purchase in Twitter is to manage multiple campaigns at the simultaneously. The top account managers and advertisers on Twitter could have up to 100 campaigns simultaneously. Initiating and running more than 10 , campaigns in Twitter at the same time could be quite a headache at the back end. This is why you need the Twitter Ads Editor becomes an important tool to master.

I'm not going to go into the process of setting the Ads Editor up; Twitter offers a great tutorial on this subject and I don't think it's worthy of my time. On ads.twitter.com you'll locate the Ads Editor in the section Tools. The tutorial video is found. You can also find info on it at business.Twitter.com. Here are some of my top tips in utilizing this tool.

1.) Always optimize for conversions In column T, you can choose your preferred optimization option. If you're not making use of the tool to develop campaign for your brand, you must always choose "Conversions". The tool focuses your web-based campaigns on driving conversions and not to simply driving clicks. It's essential for all marketing campaign that is focused on conversions.

2.) Target Bid - Auto-bid does not result in cost-effective clicks according to my experiences. Max bid doesn't drive scale in my experience. Balance that Target bid offers is crucial, and you must ensure that your DR campaigns include this option from your Ads Editor.

3.) A Test of B / C Bidding The Ads Editor permits you to assign different advertising groups to your campaigns. My advice is to alter your bid for your campaign in three ways. My experience is that bidding is often the most significant issue to scaling efficiently. Once you have an established audience and a sequence of tweets you want to test the bid, you can adjust it three different ways. An example would be that, If I decide to launch an ad campaign that targets non-purchasers who have visited my website and I want to try a bid of the price of $2.50, $2.50 as well as $3 (3 different ads groups). Under each ad group, I'd include all my different tweets.

The Ads Editor might seem complex at first, but it is vital to scaling DR advertising on Twitter. One of the fundamental principles of Twitter suggests, optimizing is an absolute requirement. The Ads Editor allows users to optimize their ads on a large scale, and quickly.

The Marketing Tactic 4, Nurture vs Acquisition

I've been talking often about direct response advertisements on Twitter. I'm not afraid to admit that it's an extremely difficult method of advertising on the platform as well. Twitter as a platform has a long way compete with other social networks. It's essential to differentiate between two types of DR and the best way to use the two to Twitter. The two forms are the acquisition marketing and nurture marketing. I suggest that at minimum 50percent of your spending is directed towards nurture marketing. In the ideal scenario, you'll get close to the 70% mark. Twitter is a social platform, which gives users to talk about the latest features to those who might have abandoned your product.

1.) Acquisition Marketing A majority of marketers are talking about acquisition when they speak of DR. It is the process of bringing new customers to your service initially. Twitter has a history of negative reviews on this site. Many advertisers feel it is too costly or time-consuming to be worth the efforts. The key to Twitter and acquisition lies in what's known as the Marketing Tactic 3. It will require volume testing and optimizations before it can scale in any way that is meaningful.

2.) Nurture marketing - That's the place where Twitter is often an effective instrument for direct response marketing. If you have a strong audience but would like to improve their interaction with your product, or get customers to buy more of your products and services, the rapid pace of Twitter can aid. I recommend that advertisers spend around 70% of time in acquisition marketing on Twitter and the remaining 70 percent on nurturing. Make use of hashtags and trending topics to reach out to users who are likely to have grown bored with your service. It's common for users to be caught by surprise to discover a brand they've had stopped engaging with on Twitter in the event that the content is targeted and targeted. If the tweets are similar to those that you've previously used to gain the information, it's unlikely to bring the results you want.

The difference between acquisition and nurture isn't easy to discern in the absence of users at the moment. In this instance I would suggest that you look into Twitter for acquiring new users, however, remember that you should make sure to install Twitter conversion pixel on your site prior to when you make any advertisements. If you concentrate your efforts to acquire users on Facebook and increase the number of users by utilizing this pixel, then you could revisit later and employ nurture ads to retarget users who may have dropped off from your site.

Chapter 10: Making The Perfect Twitter Bio

There is a lot of talk about social media and the ways you can increase the number of followers on your profile, you have to to ensure you have a great social media bio and also your perfect profile photo. We will explore the numerous ways to design your perfect profile and bio that can make you an instant Twitter winner.

There are many reasons why you should include a decent bio. In the first place, you must have a great bio, as people have a hard time remembering things. Thus, you'll only need one second to catch the attention of the person and make them follow your account. When people go to your account, they want to know more about what is your business and the things you're about and the reason they ought to care about your account. The best way to grab their attention is to write an impressive bio.

The best method to utilize your bio is to showcase the many accomplishments you've achieved and then explain to them the type of problem you are able to solve. Bios are a fantastic opportunity to make an impression from step one.

Another reason you should have an ideal bio is that you can improve the results of your search. The more appealing your bio, the greater traffic you will be able to attract and the more followers you'll draw and the more favorable the outcomes.

6.1 What is the Twitter Profile/Bio Should Be able to Do

The Twitter bio is limited to 160 characters, however you must be aware that within those 160 characters lie lots of possibilities specifically in regards to the information you have to convey. Let's take a look at points which the Twitter bio must do, and especially when it's good

It should highlight all information regarding the company, including name, the category and other details that you can alter in your profile settings.

* The bio should provide you with a means to connect with others and for them to connect with you.

It should show your personal brand and personality. your brand, and should match your voice and style to your website as well as other platforms that you're an active participant in.

* It will also help establish your PR, and it will allow the audience you are targeting to comprehend what it is that makes your brand unique and why offers better value to them.

The bio should to drive actions that are pertinent to the work you perform. The bio should assist visitors who visit your website to browse content, sign up to share information, register to attend an event or even make an purchase.

The best part is that Twitter can provide you with a couple of features you can utilize to make the process work for you.

6.2 The Key Elements of the elements of a Good Twitter Biography

There are certain aspects of a great Twitter bio that you will need to be aware of and master. Let's examine the various elements and the best ways to make the most of these elements.

i. Complete all sections

You must ensure that you fill in each of the sections that have to be filled in when making your bio. When you complete every section to ensure that users of your site get all the information they require to be able to make an informed decision.

You must customize your bio so that it's distinctive to you and your things you do. Find the appropriate header pictures and then add the name, address as well as the date of birth, theme color, and a link to your site.

The great thing about this is that photos can be used in any format between JPG and up PNG. However, the problem is that Twitter doesn't allow animated images for your profile or header image, therefore you must make use of still images.

You can save a tweet to your profile, so that when someone goes to your profile they view this tweet first. This is something important to your company or you personally.

Be sure to complete each section of the profile in a way that provides the reader with something they can relate to or identify to.

When you are creating your bio, ensure that you add something personal to your bio. The brands appear to have the most joy on Twitter let their personalities shine and included it in their bios too.

If you'd like your persona to be noticed however, you must be sure to stay consistent with what your goals are and who your business is. If the general tone you select is formal, then you have to reflect this on your profile, too.

When you are creating your bio, ensure that the information you put on the homepage contains some phrases and keywords. These are the terms relevant to your industry which will appear in search results when someone is searching for something you have to offer.

ii. Make Use of the Right Image

Do you realize that a crisp image can boost the credibility of your profile in all circumstances? The picture you upload to

Twitter is small; this is this is why you need to ensure that it is clear and high quality. Use the same image on all the social media platforms you're part of.

Don't simply throw up a photo and then think you've created the perfect starting point for your marketing requirements.

Keep in mind that everyone will see your profile photo in a particular manner. They'll swipe right or left and ignore it , or interact with your posts or refuse to join them based on the picture you post on social media. It is important to keep in mind that your profile picture is essential to your online social networking and your personal brand. The picture you choose for your profile will have a major impact on your professional career and the opportunities that arise on the platform.

Before you upload any photo, let's take a look at some of the tips to help your photo stand out from others.

iii. Show Your Face

It's obvious however, you've probably seen profile photos that do not show the face in any way. Research has shown that the face is a distinct type of image that can trigger an aspect of cognitive bias which is built in your brain person who is looking at it. You may have interests, hobbies or anything else you're a enthusiasm for - however, a profile photo is not the right place to highlight this fact.

If you're a fan of a particular interest or a hobby that you are passionate about, then put your face in the photograph and your interest in the background as you like.

It is important to stay clear of cartoon-like heads, babies as well as dogs.

iv. Frame Yourself

If you are taking a picture to post on Twitter Try to frame yourself. Most people take head shots that are far away from the camera and others are distant from their camera. Make sure that you're within the frame, to ensure that those who visit the profile are able to see the background. The face should make up an integral element of the photo.

The face should not be too distant nor too close. Let the viewer observe the face and discern it.

When your smile is too small, the viewer won't be able see your smile when your photo is presented in smaller sizes.

V. Smile

Body language is an option to express yourself in your words or actions. The way you speak can either indicate that you want to connect or not. Faces can also function in similarly. Make sure that the face of your face is warm and appropriate for the image you want to make.

A smile that is prominent in the profile photo will be associated with a positive social connection. Research has shown that those who smile on their profiles on social media are most likely to be satisfied with what they do.

Make sure to use colours that will make the face pop. If you employ colors with contrast it will cause the image stand out. It's easy and simple. Be sure to make use of colors in a proper method, or else you'll lose the significance of color contrast.

Make sure to use a simple background. You must ensure that the entire attention of the photo is your face. Backgrounds that are busy can distract from the photo, and that's not crucial. The best option is to choose the flat color of your background, or one that is basic. You can choose different backgrounds to ensure that you don't have to change your clothes.

Try a test of your profile photo. You can collect some information about your photo by making use the focus groups. This group can decide on the picture you've uploaded. Try uploading several photos to see how they compare against one another.

* Incorporate some of your brand names in the image. If you are able do so, then you must incorporate some colors from your brand into the photo to help promote the brand. Try wearing your brand colors or place the color of your brand in the background. You could also add a bit of the office on the background. You could also include a logo in the image. It may be difficult to find a good fitting, but you could attempt to add it if you think there's space. It is also possible to present your brand in a manner that, when people see

your profile photo it is clear what you stand for.

vi. Make use of an image that is clear

It is essential to ensure that your image's clarity is high enough for it to be understood. The image should reflect your face and provide an contrast to the background. Maintain this image in the same way across all the social networks where you are actively.

vii. Make the Most of the Header Image

The header image should be the most effective element of your profile image. Spend time putting certain information in the header image to ensure you can utilize the image to benefit yourself. Make sure you are creative and can showcase the character of your business or even say something about the latest products or service you're offering to the public. Make sure that you don't skip this section of your profile.

Alongside showcasing the latest merchandise or service could make use of your cover photo to promote the results of a contest or to make a seasonal announcement that you want to spread.

Here are some tips to create your perfect head image

* Be current. Make sure to highlight your products and services that are in line with the way your customer's mood is. Be sure that your branding is in line and that the colors complement the logo you've created. You can take advantage of the most recent trends in the market to market your products.

Cover images are a great way to show what you have to provide. It could be a service or product you just launched. The cover can be a great location to promote your products or services. The cover can be used to promote your current marketing campaign such as an upcoming product launch. The prominence that the image of your header is perfect for advertising ongoing marketing initiatives.

* Make use of the space on your cover image to write the name of any other preferred channels you're a part of. You may also include an address that people

can contact your. Incorporating names of different social networks within the Twitter cover photo allows Twitter users to share your company on other websites.

viii. Make use of keywords

The use of keywords in your social media marketing is essential to getting the most relevant results in search. But, don't fill your bio with keywords so that it appears like you're looking for credibility in what you write, rather than the things you're about. Utilize the various kinds of keywords readily available, such as locations keywords as well as product keywords.

ix. Add Links

To utilize using your Twitter profile to the fullest extent you can make sure to redirect users to your site and other aspects that make up your company. In order to do this, you should offer links to various areas of your business.

It is important to ensure that the link you select will direct traffic to a specific page on your site, and not just your home page. It is possible to add a link to take visitors to an event, or to a welcome page. Visitors can also be directed to the page for subscriptions to emails.

Make sure that your links give the best chance for others to follow you or be able to pass you by. The link could draw attention , and later convey a message about you and your preferences.

You must include the URL in your Twitter profile to ensure that those who are interested in finding out more about you can go to your page to find more details about your interests. The more opportunities you provide your potential client to interact to you, the more beneficial it is. People will not just come across you but also interact with you via Twitter.

If you decide to add the link to the profile of your Twitter page, you will need ensure that your website is able to handle the volume of traffic coming through. You must be able to answer any questions that may arise from the bio link.

You can include two links on your profile: one in your bio as well as one on the line on your website where it's been provided. You can also set your Twitter username an URL you would like to use.

When linking a URL another website, ensure that the website you're linking to is relevant and suitable. Don't hyperlink to your personal blog unless you are in fact you're making use of Twitter professionally. In lieu of sending a link to an individual blog, you could consider linking to a company's site or an organisation that you can then further enhance your page with regular updates, pictures videos, links, and photos. Make sure to include basic information like snail mail as well as other contact details so that you can increase communications.

x. You can use your real name

For many , their name is a difficult decision due to the fact that they do not like their name or want to go with the name of their business that they own. If you make up names create a challenge for users to connect them to other social media accounts. They also won't remember who you are or the values you promote.

xi. Add Hashtags in The Bio

The hashtags are cool but they are a great way in bringing your message to people and organisations who share similar interests as your own. When you use the hashtags into your bio, you've got the ability to attract more than a handful of followers. Here are the different methods to utilize hashtags and let them be effective in your bio.

* The Profile will be displayed in Twitter Results of Searches

If you add hashtags to the bio of your Twitter bio, you are making your profile searchable by others. People are able to find the bio with specific words and keywords.

When you add hashtags, make sure you use hashtags relevant to your business so that when someone is searching for something relevant to your business it will show up quickly.

* They share your interests

The best part about being a professional marketing professional on Twitter is the fact that you will share the things you enjoy about your life and work. Making use of the right hashtags makes it simple for you to connect with people who are interested and get the conversation moving with experts who share the same desires.

Alongside the introduction of your identity, using hashtags will allow you to connect with others in the industry that you're involved in. If you use hashtags that reflect your feelings or the things you're involved with it will allow you to network with others working in the field. This can encourage others to share their own experiences related to what their business is about. When you integrate hashtags into the bio, you must to give your brand a personality that is evident in the bio.

xii. Utilize the 160 characters

You have 160 characters you must use to make an impression on the person who visits your site. It's possible that these 160 characters will not be enough however they are enough to help get your message. However, you'll be amazed by the number of people who stop before they reach the 90 characters threshold.

If you are a marketer, do not make this error.

The ideal Twitter bio will make use of every character accessible to you. It's possible that you think you've said everything you have to say by the 100 character limit but in a practical sense, you have to keep pushing until you've reached the maximum.

It is possible to include a variety of things in your bio, including awards you've received and a call-to-action or your slogan. It isn't difficult to fill in the blanks.

Keep in mind that the purpose of your Twitter profile is to provide the full picture of your identity. This requires you to provide your personal statement of purpose at some time. You may not be able to write everything, but you are able to make it a point to mention it in passing.

Consider the main objective or mission and make it into a concise sentence. It could be difficult but it's an effective exercise that can apply wherever you choose to use it.

xiii. Don't ride the wave

You've probably come across many similar words and titles used in bios of various authors that you've seen. Be careful not to fall into the trap anytime.

If you're trying to distinguish yourself from the crowded crowd, you need to be distinctive. Your bio should have some personality. If you'd like to remain distinct, find your name to find out if the information is possible to find it.

To make your bio unique make sure to include any achievements that you've achieved during the course of your career. It is possible to include achievements from work or in the background. There is no need for it to be a huge achievement, as such. It could be something minor which you make use of when you're in this situation.

xiv. Address the Target Audience

If you run a business, you have to determine your target market and collaborate with them. A lot of people make a lot of errors with regards to the bio , as they chase after a lot of followers, most of which don't contribute to your business's marketing objectives.

You must ensure that you are specific about the platform whenever you can. You must write the bio in a manner that you are addressing customers, customers and even your fans. The bio should speak to those who are interested in the things you do and what you believe in.

xv. Don't Pretend

If you're a funny person, then show it but don't make it a priority to be funny in any way. If you've got something funny you could throw into the mix, take it to the next level. This will make you be noticed as a comedian in the formal group.

If you're not funny Don't be embarrassed to choose a basic bio that lets you stand out. If you are trying too hard to make yourself humorous, you'll make a poor impression or a bad one.

Instead, keep to the basic principles and everything will go your way.

xvi. Add an Address

Be aware that appearances are important so very much on Twitter. If you do not include the location tag in your bio, you could be missing out on what you want to achieve. That's why when you go through the top bios you'll notice that the majority of them have the location tag. they have a major purpose for having this particular tag in their bio.

6.3 Tweet Deadly Sins

We have now figured out how to best handle a Twitter bios the following step is to ensure that we know the most serious sins that people commit and how they impact how we market to other people. Here are the most common most serious sins individuals are committing.

No photo

If prospective clients decide they'd like to join your list or not, they'll initially look at your profile before making a choice. Therefore, the most costly mistake that you'll ever commit is to not include an image on your profile. The picture is the first impression a person gets about your profile. If you don't own an image, the odds of them following you diminish by an astounding 80 percent.

A Non-Personal Photograph

You may have lots of awards and other interests and you may choose to include a picture of your vehicle on the profile. However, it's not advised as it does not convey the goals you have set. Keep in mind that people are more connected to each other than inanimate objects.

Be sure to have a picture that showcases your face. The face's expression needs to be welcoming.

An Photo of Your Hero

Dad might be your idol however when you sell online the heroic qualities disappear. The people who follow they expect you to appear authentic as much as they can. If you post a picture of an object that is not animated and people tag you as an spammer.

Sexy Photos

You may have the physical assets to show that you're a professional however, you should limit the photos to other social media platforms which don't have issues with these images. It's well-known that spammers use sexually explicit photos. This can cause you to be identified as a spammer also.

A Group Photo

Be aware that people desire to be connected with others. When you decide to use a group picture as a profile picture, you'll be able to dissuade those who want to be simple. The only exceptions are married couples or a group which works together.

A Suspect Username

Keep in mind that the Twitter username will show up in any correspondence or contact that you send. Be sure that the username you choose to use won't cause you to appear to be an actual spammer. A large number of accounts using fake names are shut down much faster than if you mention your name.

Chapter 11: Twitter Networking

If you are a business owner, or a person seeking to establish a relationship with your competitors in your field, Twitter is really a excellent medium that will benefit the services of your company tremendously. There are good and bad strategies to utilize Twitter to manage systems. In this post I'll give you five essential tips on the most efficient way to organize your account on Twitter properly so to achieve the results you want.

1. Create a list of exactly the things you want to accomplish using Twitter first. If you're looking to get an enjoyable laugh, go to random to get rid of outsiders, or be enthusiastic for other people who are having the same reaction to arbitrary information, just go move ahead and do that. However, this isn't the ideal method for making the most of your business through systems-related services offered on Twitter. To do this, you must decide the exact market you're in and what area you'll need to talk to on Twitter. This is important because now you are able to

present yourself as an expert in the field you are specialized in that draws in those who require that expertise.

2. Build your Twitter profile's proximity in order that potential customers know what you're about. Use the profile of your Twitter profile to introduce anyone who is interested in becoming Twitter users who you are as well as what you are interested in or what your specialization is. Inform them about what you'd like to share, and perhaps that you are looking for like-minded people to learn from or collaborate with later If that's something you require. You can run over neighbors active and lucrative.

3. Bring an incentive to the table! Provide people with opportunities to connect with you and engage in group activities. You can ask for help, and perhaps more important, you can offer help. When you provide information, ideas, suggestions, and more about issues that people are also interested in Your Twitter services will help to create an amazing relationship as users will be able to connect with you as

the person who is knowledgeable and accommodating they may need to collaborate with. This will also result in more quality long-distance followers.

4. Make it easy to connect with specific Twitter users you think that you should be connected to. It could be described as 'Focused On Twitter Social Networking'. Similar to point 3, you need to search for the most popular Twitter organizing potential. Look them up using tools like Tweetdeck, or look up related tweets or Twitterers by entering your keyword in the search working on Twitter. Interact with people with ease and people will notice your efforts and likely want to interact with you, too.

5. Don't make use of your Twitter to promote your links continuously. This is crucial. If you "promote" a new product or service in every tweet, to ensure Twitter traffic to your websites and you'll lose followers and look like another marketer'. However the event that you combine your tolerant and enticing tweets with your sporadic marketing messages, people are

also ready to accept this, and the response to the tweets offering offers could rise.

This, again can enhance your overall standing as someone you may require assistance from.

Deep In Social Networking

There are many possibilities through your Twitter account. in the right way to market your company to current clients as well as attracting new clients and customers and even collaborating with other business owners. In any case, prior to using Twitter to conduct business it is essential to understand some essentials and nitty gritty details that must be done with a clear final goal in order to achieve success. This article will serve as an introductory Twitter preparation article to help you begin your journey.

It's a system of social interaction

Every time people use Twitter to conduct business they do not consider the social component of it. Twitter isn't just a place where you place advertisements. Users use it to interact with one another and share valuable information. It is important to be part of this group and integrate the development of your company through the management of social systems.

Meet like-minded individuals and others who are interested in the message you're trying to convey.

When you make use of Twitter to conduct your business, you'll find it is easy to interact with people who are inspired by the work you're doing. So, Twitter preparing would enable you to discover those. Be sure to use hash marks when expanding your business, and those who are truly interested will see and follow you.

Don't be too far ahead

People are seeking out interesting things and like to not be bombarded by facts about your company every day. If you're able to out-do your company, you'll only have a handful number of people following you, and that's not good. Twitter is a business tool to be present isn't something you can use in a matter of minutes, you'll need the right Twitter preparation to master these platforms.

Instead, share valuable content as well as videos and images associated with your specialization, bearing in mind your objective of gaining followers as well as keep your current fans. Maintaining your existing fans is the primary goal instead of trying to gain. If you are able to discover a way to keep your current followers happy people, new ones are likely to follow.

Attach your image to the wall

Twitter creating forms, but also let us know that the most important thing you need to remember when using Twitter for business is finding out how to stick to your brand's image and what it is that you are best at. In reality, you must increase the reach of your rivals in order to show your followers that you're working to provide them the very best. However, you should not move ahead of your rivals.

Find out how you can use Twitter creating projects to learn something new every day. This is why you must join these groups and show all of the managers within your organization to them too. The right marketing skills can take your company to the next levels.

The Effects on Business

From TVs to radios and then the internet, marketers are working to connect with the masses of viewers specifically. This helps them understand their audience better and also assists in using the models of marketing. The rise of digital media has altered the speed of marketing and an important role plays social networks and service websites. They were initially used for social interaction however, the social aspect has opened up new avenues for marketing, and specifically member marketing. SMM, or social media marketing is among the most current ways to grow your company's performance through the use of computerized media.

If you want to know which website could allow you to market your business, it would be Twitter. Twitter is the most important online marketing player. Millions and billions of people have joined Twitter from all over the world. People share their tweets with friends and are more inclined to think about the products and services available in their area. In recognition of this, a number of marketing professionals have decided to use social media marketing, which is an exciting but sensible method of promoting your company's name to the global audience.

Let's discuss the details, Twitter gives a miniaturized scale blogging platform where you can post your product's information or any other important details that you wish to communicate to your followers. Twitter is linked to sharing your expertise with others. activities, as a marketer it's essential to benefit the most you can from miniaturized blogging. in addition, you need to follow the leaders in your field. It is also possible to create your website available for visitors to visit to it on Twitter.

Marketing on Twitter can be more effective when you communicate, interact and then switch. Interact with potential customers or your target group, engage with them to gain their trust eventually, you can turn them into potential customers through essentially presenting a message to them. Every now and then, you don't have to force the pitch, they will discover that you are the person who made it.

However, I'd advise that you take a deep look at the crate, and then formulate some amazing thoughts prior to making the final presentation to your clients. Your pitch should be unique and simple but with a twist that entices your audience of followers without delay. You can also seek help with your company's CEO, or a senior official by simply asking to connect with them to give a professional view of your entire Twitter action.

Additionally, you must ensurethat your audience of viewers is always communicating with you. It is possible to connect with a large group of people by launching activities or competitions and reporting champs and the like. Twitter is a great location to grow your business provided you're following the correct path.

What is it that you are waiting for? just start!

Strategies

If you're in search of strong Twitter methods to boost your business, I've got many of them available to share with you today. The social services stage is different from any other available online on the Internet. It is unique due to the fact that it is possible to keep your information small and concise this is a great feature for the fast-paced environment that we live in. Therefore, let's look at some ways that you can boost your business through Twitter.

Concerning the Following

With that the ultimate goal is to create an impact on your business , by implementing effective Twitter strategies, you should be able to build an audience. If you remain there and believe that people will begin following you, it could be a long time for you to reach an impressive number. This way, with the intention to leave an impression to improve your business it is necessary to start tailing other people. More often than not , they will then follow you this is basically an unwritten twitter running the show.

Step-by-step instructions on how to benefit from it

Be sure to tune in, as strong Twitter methods rotate around gatherings that you follow. Based on your area of expertise it is essential to find others who are involved in the same thing. For instance, if you're developing bobblehead games; you'll have to put together an pursuing that rotates around the various games you're developing.

From a personal standpoint it's important to behave in a natural way. It's not about company and the faster you understand this, the less difficult the task will become to entice more customers. When it's time to take your business to the next level you must do more than "Hello check out this website!" Sincere to the point there are many who are likely to ignore the information. Better to include something like "Have you seen the brand new Hideki

Matsui World Series MVP notice?" Sure, you should have one but in the event of an image that's exceptional people will remember it.

The Secrets

It is important to be aware of this when using Twitter is that you only have 140 characters before it stops you. This means that in the event that you use an URL, it will be considered to be part from your character. There are a number of marketers who employ a URL marking method that make their links smaller. This means that you could include more information inside the "tweet."

If you're trying to help your marketing efforts for an article or blog gain a boost in terms of perspective to aid in the improvement of your website, you'll be important to share your link on Twitter. It doesn't matter that you're not really helping your site, you're helping it get some recognition online, so with a focus on movement, it will be able to find its way to your website.

There are many appealing Twitter strategies available to help you grow your company. If you start using the social platform your self, you'll be able to recognize various strategies on your own. The end result is that you'll be able to interact with people and develop an following. In the world of online it is essential to establishing a profitable online business.

A Guide to Utilizing Twitter to Market Your Company

This method of marketing allows you to create a name for your business and also increase visitors to your site. Social media such as MySpace, Facebook, Flickr, YouTube, Digg, and many others offer you the possibility of submitting photographs, videos, cases throws, and information regarding your business as well as the services and products that it offers. The entire procedure, however, can be very time-consuming. There's a specific case Twitter!

What is the function of Twitter? Twitter works

Twitter offers users basic social network and smaller-scale blogging stages. This is how it operates. It is best to answer this question in 140 characters-"What's going on in your life?" These messages are short and easy to write, and they are referred to as tweets! Your tweets will be immediately at hand displayed on your profile and be sent to users whom you have been "tailing" your profile. When you're using Twitter you'll find people on the internet "tailing" you , and they'll also being "tailing" those users. "Following" means that at any time you add a new post to one of your contacts' profiles, you'll get refreshed. In addition, if you leave a comment that you want to get "took following." Therefore, the more people who follow you, the greater chance your business be introduced. However, expanding your business isn't simply about adding more people to your list of friends. It's about assembling your fan base effectively. Before you start "tweet"ing it's important to learn more about ways in which it works. Twitter people group operates and how to promote your company by using the platform. Here are some guidelines that will help you start.

Better Marketing
Starting with enlisting, organizing short-term events and promoting your event to your followers, to organizing contests and giveaways and compensating Twitter reliability and incorporating metadata into tweets, and keeping an constant eye on Twitterverse There are some unwritten guidelines that will aid you in developing your business by using Twitter. Be aware of these guidelines.

1. Make yourself noticed: Twitter is an awesome platform to connect with new people and create an organization. A great way to ensure that you're heard through:

2. Follow-up with those who can be relevant to your company is essential in contrast to creating a large number of hyperlinks. It is suggested to include your current and former customers, as well as people who are in a position in an industry that is similar to yours.

Incorporating Contacts Incorporating Contacts: If you are a member with LinkedIn or Facebook the best option is to create connections on Twitter. It is also possible to add contacts directly from Gmail, Hotmail, Yahoo mail or your own personal address book.

Reducing the Followers/Following Rate There must be a balance between the people who follow you as well as the general population that you go after. If you have a lot of people following you , and you do not follow them, they'll be sure to stop following you. If, however, the change occurs, you'll be viewed as a spammer trying to increase the number of people who follow him. One of strategies you can use to prevent this change in mind include:

Develop slowly: Instead of adding new members all at once an ideal approach is to start by adding 50 people and then sit close to them until they tail you back. Once they have a tail You can then add another 50 people.

Use the "Companion or Follow" tool It is suggested to use tools such as "Companion or Follow" which allow you to verify your identity to identify who is following you and that you aren't following.

Do not stop following You should not follow other people and then stop tailing them when they start following you, you'll get considered spammer.

Keep a safe separation of Automated Functions: Automated capacities appear to be robots. Remember that you're communicating with humans not robots. People need to listen the voice of you, and not to the voice of the robot. So, refrain from using the auto-answer or auto-take-after functions which are offered via Tweet Adder.

Collaboration: When you simply communicate announcements, you'll not get the respect of many followers, and this isn't helpful for your company. It is essential to reserve the opportunity to interact and engage with your fellow Twitter followers. Make it personal.

3. Get started pitching: Many people who are new Twitter users have started an attempt to lead you to a site they require you to go to. It doesn't work for very long. One of the most effective formulas you can employ to market your business via Twitter is:

4. Associate Converse - Convert It is first necessary to interact with the people who are a significant portion of whom don't know, so start talking to them until the point that you have a chance to win on their faith, then present a pitch. In fact, it could be the case that you must not to pitch them. They might be looking at them. Think clearly: Before making a pitch to prospective clients, it's advised to think about and create strong and compelling thoughts about your business. Present these ideas to your clients and solicit their opinion. This is certainly superior to an online survey or a vote. It can make them become a crucial part of your business's endeavor.

5. Invite your CEO to join to be a part of social media is an enormous undertaking

as it's extremely time-consuming. Your CEO will in no doubt have no time to write a blog, in addition to respond to questions, messages. Also, you must acknowledge the demands of your companions. "Tweet"ing however it is a distinct. If your CEO is able to make a quick message to you, then he is likely to use Twitter. Twitter is a tiny scale blog stage, gives your CEO the possibility to use this social media for marketing and PR tool.

6. Include Value: Simply asking to have people follow you isn't enough. You need to provide them with the incentive to follow you. The best way to do this is by providing valuable information, such as advice, responses to people's questions along with links and amazing deals only for your followers. In time, you become a prominent member of the Twitter community that will increase your followers. One way to boost your Twitter account include posting amazing deals, offers or arrangements: Twitter is an extraordinary way to advertise unique deals within a matter of seconds to a large

number of users. Presenting live updates of events or gatherings If you're a part of a public event or have your own company event, you could use Twitter to issue a minute prior announcement, or to inform crowds of people about fascinating events taking place. It is an excellent time-sensitive marketing tool.

7. Blend Business With Pleasure Marketing your products and service isn't enough. You must also market yourself. This means that people have to get to know your side. To do this, go forward and enjoy a wonderful time. Instruct people about your choices and interests, and other aspects. It will make your customers closer to you. You'll get their attention and trust, which is important for your business.

8. Unwavering loyalty: Businesses have realized that what is unique in comparison to other methods to enhance the worth of their business is to reward customers who have passed on their buying methods to their families. If you are an Twitter customer, you will find ways to reward the faithfulness of those who are sending out

information about your business to their friends on Twitter users. However you need to ensure that they're sending the right message to improve your image.

9. Study the market: Keeping close watch on your rivals in the same field and the people that they compete with is essential. You will need a substantial investment, and you'll have to make an inventory of them to ensure to keep an eye on these. It is possible to create this list by using tools like Twitter Lists. Also, try to stay clear of trend-setters, influencers, and also those who soften the news in your market. Find out about their conclusion of the week workouts and what they must speak about their image. This will help you display signs of improvement in regards to what you're competing to and also what you and your customers need.

10. Groups of people who are interested in your business The most appealing aspect of Twitter is that it allows you to communicate with any person anywhere in the world through tweets of 140

characters. However, you must ensure that you use this tool to target smaller groups that are important to your company. Promoted Tweets can be a good alternative. Although Promoted Tweets may not be live for all clients They do aid business users in targeting their tweets to specific groups of individuals, elevating their business to a previously unheard of scale. However, you should make use of this tool with aplomb. You'll gain the trust of your crowd of friends if you show them that their demands begin the process and not yours.

11. Add your own metadata In the near future, Twitter will give you the opportunity to add metadata i.e. note areas, labels, and notes. This will give the business community the chance to label tweets which originate on their websites, connect their own identifiers, find strategies to reward loyalty and roll out enhancements on guest's notes behavior on the spot Twitter behavior, and other options.

12. Create a brand for yourself: Creating a brand on Twitter is imperative to create a base of supporters. Here are some ideas to consider.

Individual marking Personal marking is just crucial as marking your business. This can be accomplished by focusing the attention on you Twitter address and the biodata you have entered.

Get your Twitter handle registered Names for space are sought-after and are now proving to be difficult to find and also expensive. If you don't have your own space name, you're placing your brand and business at risk. When your name for your area was taken, you will not be able to retrieve it. Similar is the case with Twitter. Account names on Twitter are currently being treated as domain names. So, just go forward and claim the Twitter username!

Create a account of the client: The very first step in marking your own profile is to fill in your profile as a client. If you want to attract followers, you require an excellent profile. If your profile isn't authentic, customers won't even take a second look.

In this regard, before you create your client profile, go through various profiles and websites and follow an organization that is similar to yours. Don't advertise yourself as a professional unless you're one. It is always more beneficial to broaden your scope of skills and interests, and establish yourself as a professional in light of them.

Focus on the Twitter base: After completing the profile of the user The time is now to focus on your Twitter base. This will allow you to expand your picture on Twitter. Your followers will be given an entire experience. Twitpaper as well as Twitterimage are two sites that help you build an individual foundation. It is recommended that you connect similar colors, logos and design in your Twitter foundation that you've created to create your company's or personal website. Don't include information that's not listed within the profile of your Twitter profile.

Be the leader of your organization One of the most effective ways to mark your company is by placing your business in front of your. This creates an image for the company as well as provides you with the identity and appearance to abide by it.

13. Create an Twitter marketing plan There are several elements that you need to integrate to help market your site.

Email signature Add your Twitter handle in your email signature is helpful. It ensures that with every email you send you will be able to get another fan.

Websites for corporate or personal websites The addition of your Twitter delivery to your own or corporate website is an additional way to promote your website.

Blog post: An additional great option to boost the Twitter profile of through your blog. People who read blogs are likely to think of Twitter. It is possible to put your Twitter username in any of your sidebars on your blog and add it to your blog posts.

Email bulletins: If you send out email pamphlets, then you may discuss Twitter in them or add it to your personal profile, so that every email will be linked with your profile.

Introductions: When you introduce yourself, a smart idea is to include your Twitter account in the final slide of your introduction. Invite people to follow you.

Business card: Another way to combine is to include the Twitter username on your card.

Article writing When you write an article for publication or guest post on an online news site or blog make sure that your byline includes the Twitter handle. Twitter handle.

14. You will be able to establish yourself as a professional In the process of constantly expounding your knowledge on a specific topic, people will quickly recognize your name, remember your name, and begin to follow you. Also, be part of Q&A sessions in which you are able to respond to any questions your followers might be asking, as well as enhance your expertise in the subject.

15. Utilize applications from outside There are many Twitter applications, but only a handful can help you build your personal brand. These apps aid you find people you

can create a network with, stay in touch with people in your field which will save you time as well as enhance your content. The applications you can use include:

Twellow It is an Twitter business index management system which allows you to find people in your field that you can follow and join.

Twhirl: This app is a constant saver. If tweeting takes more than 60 seconds, then Twhirl reduces that time to less than 10 seconds.

Twellow: With this app you'll be able to keep track of your image's fame. You'll receive warnings via email whenever your image is mentioned on Twitter.

HashDictionary: Keep on your guard against discussions that contain hashtags. Twitter.

Tweetmeme: This app allows you to create a catchy tweet on your blog. This allows you to go through the possibility of effortlessly share your content.

Twitter Grader It is a site which places you in the relation to the impact you make on

Twitter. It is a chance to try the calculation.

Ping.fm This application you'll be able to save much time and effort by messaging all of your social networks in a double.

Tweetlater: By using this app you can create tweets that will be distributed later.

16. Create a frame for a tweet "Driving group for force"

There are a variety of groups of users on Twitter that have similar views and interests and are moving forward by retweeting each other. They always support each other and help each other to become in a way that is more effective. These gatherings are known as "Driving Force Groups." There are a few applications on Twitter that you could use to organize these gatherings. This includes:

GroupTweet: Using this app it allows users to organize gatherings and share their messages to one another using the use of instructions which can be sent to the group's Twitter account.

Facebook Groups on Twitter: This site lets you identify your followers and put them in various gatherings. It is then possible message these groups instead of sending them to each individual separately.

7 Reasons You Should Take Action

If you own an unincorporated business and don't making use of Twitter and Facebook, I'd like to know the reason? It seems like pretty much everyone else around the globe with access to the internet or a wireless network is.

Twitter is, by all accounts, following the same pattern as blogs followed. At first, it was a couple of users, and only for private use (please!) There is a growth of jobs. Then a sudden arousal by companies that something is taking place in the distant future and it could be worth pursuing it.

It's a good idea, despite the hassle, as 47 percent of those who follow after a company's name on Twitter will likely visit that site of the company. It is easy to see for 65.8 percent of U.S. organizations are currently making use of Twitter to promote their business (Twitter Statistics are for Businesses).

Do you remember the switch records of Letterman? If you think about it this is one of reasons why you should connect your company to Twitter and start tweeting, from the most basic to essential.

Small businesses should be using Twitter because every other person is using it.

The person in charge of the hotel on the other side of the road. The scene designer. The proprietor of the shoe store. Additionally, a lot of large companies such as Dell, HP, AT&T and Microsoft? In reality 74 percent of the 2013 Inc 500 organizations utilize Twitter and 377 of 2013's Fortune 500 organizations have a corporate Twitter account ((Twitter Statistics to Businesses). A business's presence is on Twitter is a hot.

Twitter is an excellent source of optics.

Making use of Twitter can prove that your business is interested in social media, and is evidently an "with-it" type of dress that people might be interested to work with.

It's not enough to have a website anymore. (Figure out the steps to create an effective Facebook and Twitter Social Media Plan for Your Business.)

Twitter is a simple way to share the message.

In the event that your potential and existing clients to be using Twitter You can immediately send them your information regardless the nature of it being an announcement, other item, an exclusive arrangement, or an upcoming event that they are engaged with.

Furthermore, since businesses can market on Twitter it's much easier to connect with potential customers you're trying to reach.

Twitter can help you keep your job as well as in the market.

Twitter offers you the chance to learn what other users are saying. With Twitter Search, you can see what others are talking about on the subject matter, which allows you to keep your ears to the ground for information about your business and opposition.

Twitter lets you improve your image.

Participating on Twitter (that is, using it to interact with other users rather than simply posting announcements of products) you are able to display and create the kind of images that entice your prospective customers, and improve your profile. (Keep that in mind: the exchange of information is not a one-way process.)

Twitter is an amazing system tools for services.

The presence on Twitter gives the chance to interact with a myriad of people Some of whom aren't likely to have the chance to chat with other people. Furthermore these people might be the exact people you've been looking for, the people you're looking to start a business with, source products from, or even sign a contract with.

The primary reason for your company should make use of Twitter - is that Twitter offers you the an opportunity to attract customers.

Sharing information about your product or benefits could be the undisputed benefit.

However, Twitter additionally gives you another avenue for listening to and getting answers about your customers and their opinions or dislike about your business and how they feel about your image, what suggestions they have for improvement and what their favorite products are and why... A wide variety of information you can utilize to make your company more productive.

There you go. In essence, Twitter can provide your business a new avenue to help and attract your current and future customers every chance to do this is worth investigating.

It is important to make sure that you're using Twitter properly to grow your business, to ensure that you don't come across as spammers and damage your company's reputation.

The Truth About Purpose

In this multi-part series on Twitter marketing for independent businesses We'll walk you through the tips, advice and best practices for making the most of

Twitter for your company. If you follow these easy steps that you make, your leads and followers will grow substantially. To a certain extent We explained the reason Twitter is an essential step that every private company should include in their arsenal of marketing equipment. In this article we will discuss the reasons behind business.

Twitter is primarily a broadcasting Site, so your focus is on building and maintaining a community, as well as promoting CONTENT to your community so that they can eventually upload it to your website or blog.

The motivation behind Twitter to be used for small Business Marketing:

The stage for listening: Twitter is an amazing location to stay in touch with the discussion on social media. You can view other people who are active and follow the conversations among users as well as their reactions to events of the moment. This lets you know what's going on in the mind of your market target and react quickly to their needs and preferences.

Give Your Brand a Personality One of the most unique social media platforms, Twitter is the place where you have the opportunity to offer your personal brand and your friends the chance to let their reflect the culture. You've likely seen Twitter described as the mix drinks mix of all social media. It is undeniably true that Twitter is a platform that is awe-inspiring and enthralling with brief conversations happening between colleagues. Be aware that individuals interact with each other so the private interactions that occur on Twitter becoming a significant source of income for every business.

Demonstrate your learning and mastery Like other social media platforms, Twitter is a gathering to give an incentive by giving advice or directions, or asking questions and allowing your market's attention to recognize your brand as a thought-leader in your field.

Give real-time updates: Twitter empowers you to instantly update your clients, followers and customers about what's happening with you and your company. At a personal level, Twitter can be instrumental in quickly distributing updates across your entire organization.

Link people to your blog or website: Twitter is an extraordinary method of communicating with people when you have something new to communicate. It lets you create an impressive feature and provide directly to your blog, or to any specific page on your site. The majority of people who follow your blog would have decided to let your blog use the RSS channel, but when they come across interesting content on Twitter they will be able to easily of a hassle browse to your blog. Take Twitter as a busy Parkway and your content as off-ramps to your blog or website.

Gain through the lowest barrier to entry: Twitter is truly one of the least obstructed barriers of interacting with other people. It is easy to follow or unfollow someone who has no formal invitation.

Twitter was founded in 2006, and has since increased to the number of users to 200 million and 1.6 billion searches per day. It's the perfect social media platform for entrepreneurs to connect with their customers over time and gain the loyalty of customers.

Yet, many business owners are aware that Twitter as being, at a extent, complicated when they first they began to look closer. Twitter also has its own rules and best practices that aren't like those of Facebook and LinkedIn which often leave owners of businesses confused and overwhelmed. But, with some time and effort, Twitter can be an extremely effective tool for business marketing with the eight reasons laid below.

1. Customer Service

Customers at times require an immediate response to a question... .Twitter can be the ideal platform to do this. If the issue or query can be addressed within the 140-character limit, frequently it will be dealt with and disseminated within 140 words or less.

1. 2. Management of Notoriety

Twitter allows you to efficiently monitor the estimate of your image, its products and services. There you can express gratitude to the person singing your praises or even mediate and try to make a client who was disappointed happy again, making maintenance of your client a important benefit of Twitter

2. 3. Lead Generation

Twitter is an easy platform to publish any esteem-based information, such as the blog posts of your organization eBooks, online courses, and other publications as well as other essential inbound marketing material that can influence your image to stand out from the crowd and become an industry expert. If you're using Twitter as an instrument for assessing lead age make sure you're using points of arrival that detect the data of a lead prior to providing access to the material.

3. 4. Market Intelligence and Research

Twitter is an amazing way to gain the understanding of your customers quickly. Are you wondering if your customers would be interested in receiving deals, particular data, content, or emails? Have them ask on Twitter. Are your customers more inclined to downloading coupons that they can print out or a coupon that could be used as part of a shopping basket or both? You can ask them on Twitter.

6. Accurate Research

Twitter information is read by everyone of course , and most companies that market via Twitter do not guarantee their tweetsare secure, therefore Twitter is the ideal platform to observe your competitors. Make use of an outside app like Hootsuite to create the stream and monitor the watchwords and notifications of your competition.

7. Catchphrase Phrase Opportunities

Another effective method of drawing to the attention of an audience is to use the propelled look option to search for tweets using watchword phrases for a unique rare chance to meet people who could benefit from your service or product. For example, if you receive a tweet that reads "searching for an electrician" and your company involves plumbing services, then you could look up these watchword phrases in tweets with an outsider program and then mediate.

8. Advance Other Social Networks

If you're running sweepstakes on Facebook then share it with Twitter. If you've just refreshed your company's profile on LinkedIn and want to share it with your followers, do so via Twitter. If you get a good response to the announcement you made on Facebook and Twitter, you can share the news on Twitter and encourage your followers to share their feelings. By advancing on different platforms, you allow your followers to get familiar with your various systems and increases your awareness.

4. 8. Make Your Brand Unique Brand

One of the most lucrative reasons to use Twitter is the fact that it lets your account to have an identity. People want to interact with each other, not with businesses. Your Twitter's voice should be authentic and friendly. If you can do this requirement, you'll have lasting customers who may be able to become brand advocates.

Provide a photo of your smiling associate or share a photo of your stall at an expo or ask a question which evokes a response from your followers. You can also raise the value of your offer on your fans, post your most convincing argument and why you enjoy it, be excited for the release of your latest product or re-tweet an individual's thoughtful comment about your photo and express appreciation towards them, join in conversations about your specialization and share a video from your most recent event. This is the true impact of using social media for marketing as well as Twitter. you will be viewed as credible, valuable and influence customers to buy your goods and services.

How have you seen Twitter as a valuable tool for marketing?

Do you need help staying informed about Twitter? Honeybee Social can offer assistance. We are able to completely manage your Twitter as your representative, or co-supervise the process together, or advise with you on the best methods, effective procedures and marketing campaigns.

Better Marketing

With an estimated 200 million people sending out a similar number of small-sized blogs (roughly) frequently, Twitter is positively a efficient channel for communicating. However, this social system service isn't just for teenagers or celebrities posting their day to routine activities. The power that is Twitter as a tool for marketing has been recognized by a variety of entrepreneurs who are using it to allow their business to grow. Since it costs nearly nothing to advertise products on Twitter businesses that are independent ought to make use of this platform for increasing their online marketing efforts.

How Twitter can benefit private companies?

Here are some factors that highlight the reasons Twitter is crucial for private firms and the ways they can make money through it.

Interact with clients

Twitter is a plethora of users, and more are joining it regularly, which makes it one of the most popular sites to find prospective customers. Smaller companies that are able to target a specific market or people who are who reside in a particular area may make use of Twitter to join with them. In addition, companies can also interact with their existing customers and communicate with them in order to get information what the company's brand is perceived on the market.

Manufacturing relationships

Be sure to limit your marketing posts regarding deals or an advancement to a foundation, since the excessive number of marketing posts can hinder your efforts at creating a positive image. Additionally, refrain from sending too many tweets in the same direction, all being considered, the action can be viewed as spam.

Note your mindfulness

Massive brands need no introduction to gain followers. In any event entrepreneurs who require more attention to their brand or product must use Twitter to build their brand's image. People prefer to interact with someone rather than an image and unless it's notable. This is why, in the case that you have an unrelated business that is in its infancy it is better to create an individual profile initially, then make an account for your company. Once you have gained confidence from your fans then you can introduce them with your profile and create a profile to draw attention to it.

New items for marketing

The primary reason companies should make use of Twitter is to communicate with prospective customers and promote their products. Once you've set up an account for your company it is possible to utilize the Twitter account to promote new products under the brand or offering. Products that are new, and especially ones that your customers like, gain more attention via these social system websites more than via traditional marketing channels.

Give data

The speed of news on Twitter is faster than on television or radio. You can use your Twitter account to make important announcements and provide any information that your customers need to be aware of. While a radio or television announcement could perform the same job to yours, Twitter is less expensive and your message can be distributed to a wide range of people in a short amount of time.

Review and suggestions

Twitter is an excellent way to interact with clients and promoting your products. However, it's also a powerful tool to gather feedback from clients and their opinions on your business's products and services. Simply follow the discussions regarding your business products and you'll discover the solutions you need without asking. If you're looking for something particular you want to know it is possible to do that by asking customers directly or gathering details from your records.

See online fame

Apart from gaining customer feedback, you can also make use of Twitter to study and analyze the content being posted regarding your product and your acquaintances in general. People use Twitter to share what they are doing and what they think about everything and everything. Therefore, it is possible that a disgruntled customer or competitor could use the small-scale blogging website to draw attention to your products. Monitoring Twitter conversations that include your picture will help you deal with the situation and handle your online reputation with a professional manner.

Lift deals include amazing offers and cash back

It doesn't matter if you're an established brand or a small business, a free vouchers for rebates or gifts will always attract more people. A notable method to inform your customers about the various unique rebates and limited time deals being regulated by your business is to tweet on the offer. Coupon codes that expire without notice or other special offers to clients who visit your page can be a great way to attract more customers and build online fame for your business image.

Be on the lookout for rivals

Utilizing tools such as Twitter Search can be an amazing way to monitor your status on Twitter and to monitor the actions of your rivals and notoriety. Learning about your competition will help you design your marketing strategies and avoid bots which could affect your company.

Twitter is a popular social media platform.

If you notice a lot of popularity on Twitter and you'll have the ability to see the benefit of your tweets becoming into a worldwide phenomenon. A Twitter message is retweeted an unlimited number of times, meaning that any interesting or valuable message you share could be shared with many Twitter users in a short time. This technique, when combined with your advertising or time-bound tweets can yield amazing results.

Promote your blog for your business

If you've got an organizational blog that is part of your SEO methods the best way to promote it is to use Twitter. If you believe that the information contained on the blog will be appreciated by your followers you can tweet the URL to promote the blog. This will increase traffic to your blog and can make your blog's content go viral if people find the content useful.

The most appealing aspect of Twitter is that it's completely free, which makes it the ideal marketing solution for businesses that are not independent. Whatever the case, it is important to make sure you use this useful tool correctly and to keep a safe distance from it, so that you don't go in your favor and also recognition.

The most efficient method to use Twitter to increase pedestrian activity is to use Twitter

Twitter is a continuous extension of your following on the internet and the physical storage space that you require more customers to visit. Check out these guidelines for the most efficient way to use Twitter to increase pedestrian traffic.

Twitter Contests on Twitter: Hosting

Do you believe that you're searching for the most unique method to promote your online business and reach the most people? You might want to consider coordinating the possibility of a Twitter challenge! The benefits of the Twitter challenge can generate huge followings as well as the added benefit of highlighting your business' name before people who are not. Participants during your contest will remember your name, the services you have to offer, and will be able to verify whether you're offering every day something else. When you put your energy into Twitter At some point or when you are motivated, you'll be faced with one or two challenges. Every day, people join the site and sponsors offer iPads, iPods, TVs and just about everything you could imagine.

What is the reason they do this? The answer is simple, they work. Before you even begin a challenge, make sure you read the rules on Twitter. It is essential that you adhere to the guidelines to your challenge with a particular purpose to protect your Twitter account as well as the track record of the contestant. It is equally important to decide on the marketing effects you want to avoid this particular challenge. In other words do you think you're attempting to increase your mark or declare that you're actually seeking an increase in followers to the Twitter profile? How will you conduct the contest, using Twitter? Perhaps you'll need to manage the challenge on your website and then promote the challenge via Twitter? These questions should be answered before you begin.

After taking look at the rules decide the amount of your prize and you'll be able to launch your own twitter challenge. The next step is to come up with an amazing prize. This is the reason why the general public is coming in and will be returning. If you aren't sure the funds to buy that fantastic product, look for a helper to assist you. Make sure to mention his name throughout the contest to give him an advantage. If you are able to offer an amazing prize, consider offering it to a person and also. When you present the prize, think about the best way to do it and what you'll say to the majority of those who did not take home the prize, regardless of how much you have. Make sure you have advancements prepared for the next challenge and ensure that you inform your followers on Twitter when you'll need to look for it when it's due to occur. Enjoy yourself by completing your challenge. Be unique and you'll want to be able to do your challenges all the time.

Best Branding

Twitter is one of the most rapidly developing social systems tools to help users with their services. Since its launch in March 2006, Twitter has grown in rapid growth and especially in this way, during the last year. With over 45 million active users (not all of them remain active) Twitter is a device that is revolutionizing the way businesses operate.

It's helping to improve communication by speeding up the process. It's making it easier and less burdensome, making it more efficient to interact with people, organizations as well as associations. It's a free tool its simple and light method, in the context of the idea of blogging on a smaller scale, has forever altered the landscape of being online.

With messages restricted in 140 characters and in this way, the less extensive blog users are constrained to convey their needs, requirements and desires. The implications of this software for businesses are immense.

How can companies be able to make the most of this powerful tool? Let's look at the possibility of doing this. Twitter is a great tool to use to aid in your overall mark management for your organization. First of all importance, choosing your Twitter username is vital. The Twitter username can be limited to 15 characters, so choose wisely. Use your real name, not one that's funny or clever especially if you're trying to promote your business's professional name.

Although many people occasionally visit the Twitter pages of clients It's an ideal idea to make sure that you identify your page with your company's logo, color styles, colors and everything else that is a reflection on your name and the things you do. A well-constructed Twitter base is one of the most important methods to convey your image.

The bio on your Twitter profile is important. You only have 160 characters to promote your profile and describe what you are doing. Likewise, incorporate a decent expert photo. If you're not an individual business, you can use the logo of your company.

It is important to include a hyperlink to your company's website and your location. While a lot of people do their work on the internet, there are many who require interaction with you eyes to your.

Once you've established your Twitter's point of entry Check each one of the links and make sure it's working. This is the first phase of highlighting your profile on Twitter.

Building Status
1. Tweet about Your Business

Establishing your company through Twitter is extremely easy. In the event that, for instance, you're working on an additional item it is best to tweet about the subject. You can post, "I am caught up writing an eBook for an exhibition." Other Tweeps will be enthralled at your effort. Some might purchase it after it's finished.

However, be careful when playing this game. Talking about your profession or work is commonplace, but be careful not to convey it to people who are a bit off. It is also possible to include your website's address on your profile and ensure that the site has sufficient information about your job. This will provide you with the best chance of bringing more clients.

2. Twitter about the Product You Tweet About

It's possible to conclude that you are driving another thing? Tweet about it at least once a day , or more frequently if needed. When you tweet about it, include information about how people could benefit from this product. For example, if you know you've made web design layouts, you can Tweet: "Chipping away at making websites that will allow people who are not experts to create professional-looking pages." You could also post a tweet on how the product is doing: "I am getting positive feedback from customers who purchased my layouts." Tweeps will surely be interested in your product.

Tweet about your item in different times, based on the fact that Tweeps look over their accounts in various situations. However, you shouldn't just tweet about your product. Incorporate a number of tweets from social media within your company tweets, and make sure you reply to Tweets from other Twitter users. If you do not comply, other Twitter users may view your tweets as spam.

3. Tweet about your blog posts

Distribute gifts related to your business or product on your blog. Tweet the link to your followers along with brief descriptions of the blog article. The content ought to be useful to your followers.

Here's a tweet that serves as the illustration "How you can build a website in 10 Simple Steps" followed by a link. If users find the information you've given them to be beneficial and useful, they will become interested in your service and also.

4. Twitter Your Affiliate Links

Twitter could allow you to earn higher commission checks. First, you must gather all the links to your associates together in one place. It is now possible to tweet these hyperlinks at Twitter people who're seeking the data. This means you could offer your Clickbank products or receive recommendations to the program.

How can you identify Twitter users that might be interested in your referral hyperlinks? Search for a word that is associated by an item you're trying to sell on Twitter Search. For example, you may want to publish an eBook about the most efficient method of finding jobs. Simply search the catchy phrase "discover work" in Twitter Search and it will show all the tweets posted by Twitter users seeking employment. You will be able respond to these tweets with information on the service you're offering , or provide referral links to businesses that you work for. This is not a way to spam anyone in this instance. The data you provide is to those who are searching for that information! You have recently tried to assist by providing data that is of great value. The links you've shared could be the exact that the Twitter user is looking for. If they are able to successfully sign up at the website you've suggested and they either light up your profile or ignore your suggestion. Then, you'll be able to suggest a different organization or product. This strategy will permit you to have the most successful marketing with partners.

www.ingramcontent.com/pod-product-compliance
Lightning Source LLC
Chambersburg PA
CBHW071123050326

40690CB00008B/1318